W9-CGY-839

Donated by
William C. Mitchell
BUCHANAN LIBRARY
George Mason University

PRICES, MARKETS AND WELFARE

PRICES, MARKETS AND WELFARE

DAVID COLLARD

PRICES, MARKETS AND WELFARE

Crane, Russak & Company, Inc.
New York

Published in the United States by

Crane, Russak & Company, Inc.
52 Vanderbilt Avenue, New York, N.Y. 10017

Printed in England

Library of Congress Catalog No. 72–85181

ISBN 0–8448–0071–6

© 1972 Copyright David Collard

CONTENTS

CONTENTS

INTRODUCTION

This book is about the relationship between microeconomic theory (or price theory) and economic policy. It is neither a textbook of price theory nor a handbook of applied economics. I am aware that for this very reason the book may fall between two stools. But I do feel many of the most interesting and important questions about the theoretical underpinnings of economic policy are pushed to one side in the student's early years only to be brought up by more senior (and possibly graduate) students and then on a mathematical and welfare theoretic plane. I hope that first and second year students, specialists and non-specialists alike, will gain something from a treatment of these issues at a fairly rudimentary level.

The book falls into three main sections. At the beginning of each of these there is a short statement of what is to follow.

The reader will probably be aware of the conventional distinction between positive and normative statements. To say that a fall in import duties will cause imports to rise is to make a positive statement (which may or may not be true). To say that import duties *ought* to be reduced is to make a normative statement. It implies value judgements or judgements about ends. Rather early in the book it becomes clear that some apparently innocuous statements are in fact 'value loaded'; one has to be vigilant. Nor is it entirely satisfactory to separate questions of income distribution (normative) from questions of efficiency (positive). Acts of policy aimed at increasing efficiency or raising real income will have redistributional effects and acts of redistribution may have an impact on real income.

I must make the customary genuflection to the hypothetico-deductive view of *the* scientific method as setting up hypotheses, drawing out their implications (or predictions), testing them and rejecting those that are found wanting. No doubt this is more or less what happens, or what methodologists imagine to happen. I shall not, however, in this book, be 'testing' theories but rather picking up the links between statements about economic policy and 'value judgements' about ends.

Essentially the book is about prices. Prices are traditionally associated with free markets and private enterprise. Indeed the first part of the book deals with the properties of competitive equilibrium and the conditions required for laissez-faire to be a 'good thing'. But prices are essentially signals for decentralised decision-making. They can, to some extent, be stripped of their ideological trappings. One then turns back to competitive equilibrium for hints about the conditions of efficient production and exchange. Thus the second part of the book deals with price and output policies in the public sector of a mixed economy and the role of prices and markets in implementing an overall economic plan. The third and last section of the book is rather more *ad hoc* in nature. It discusses some of the ways in which policy makers might intervene positively to achieve their objectives.

The book omits to treat in detail whole sets of topics that might normally be covered. It is hoped that the reader who is new to economics will read it in conjunction with one of the excellent major texts now available (see Bibliography). On the other hand it does treat a number of topics which one would not expect to find in an introductory text, for example, externalities, second-best, market socialism and cost-benefit analysis.

ERRATA

Page 3, line 12. For 'factors' read 'actors'.
Page 6, the formulae should read:

$$E_d = \frac{-\triangle Q_d}{Q_d} \div \frac{\triangle P}{P}$$

$$E_s = \frac{\triangle Q_s}{Q_s} \div \frac{\triangle P}{P}$$

PART I

MARKETS

PART 1

MARKETS

1 COMPETITION

The five chapters of this section are concerned, one way or another, with competition. What is competition? How do the laws of supply and demand work? Is competition efficient? Is it desirable?

Perfect competition can be said to exist when:

(1) The good or factor service being considered is homogeneous. One unit of it is a perfect substitute for any other unit. Consequently the same market price must rule for all units.

(2) The number of producers and consumers of each good or factor service is very large and there is no collusion between them. Each must therefore take the market price as given.

(3) The present market price must be known with certainty and all factors in the market must have firm expectations about future prices.

Additionally, in order for any competitive system to work, it is necessary that:

(4) Each firm faces a rising curve of marginal costs (see Chapter 2).

(5) Each consumer's subjective demand price falls (other things being equal) (see Chapter 2).

(6) Markets both singly and taken together behave in a stable way.

(7) Prices are not rigid.

Further, in order for it to be efficient (see definition in Chapter 4),

(8) Marginal externalities must be taken into account (see Chapters 4 and 7). Notice that monopoly, increasing returns, etc., have been excluded by the above assumptions.

Finally, for competitive equilibrium to be optimal,

(9) The distribution of income and resources must be 'just'.

(10) The preferences of individuals must count.

All of these assumptions are contentious, others absurdly unrealistic. But the welfare economist has a love-hate relationship with his competitive model. Perfect competition can be shown to lead to 'efficiency' (see Chapter 4). But real world competition is not perfect, therefore we cannot be at all sure that it is efficient, let alone optimal. Thus the competitive model can be used to establish a *prima facie* case against laissez-faire. Further, it can be shown that the 'neo-classical liberal' solution, which attempts a clearcut separation of efficiency from redistributional questions, cannot be sustained (see Chapter 4).

Chapter 2 is a simple statement of some elementary supply and demand theory. It is hoped that most readers already have a grounding in the subject and that the somewhat sketchy presentation of important details will suffice. The behaviour of the principal actors in the market is considered and it is attempted to give some idea of the inter-relationships in a system of general economic equilibrium.

Chapter 3 is an account of the rôle of interest rates and time. This discussion is intended to be useful in itself and can stand alone. But it is of use in Chapter 4, and in some later sections.

Chapter 4 presents a 'basic theorem' of welfare economics: a theorem about competition and efficiency. It then considers the conditions needed to move from positive to normative statements about competitive equilibrium.

Chapter 5 is a little longer than I had first intended. It shows how, in the past, economists have regarded the rôle of free markets. Essentially it is a critique both of the value judgements commonly employed and of the models used.

2 PRICES AND MARKETS

The two main sets of actors in a market economy are firms and households. They come together in several markets sometimes acting as suppliers, sometimes as demanders. In each of these markets equilibrium price and quantity are determined by the forces of supply and demand. Because of the close relationship between the perfectly competitive model and many important welfare propositions, I shall assume, to begin with, that competitive conditions prevail.

Suppose that a single homogeneous commodity is bought and sold in a unified market. Let each buyer and seller be a price-taker, i.e., he must take the ruling price as given. Consider a supply and demand diagram as drawn in Figure 1. For the present it is assumed

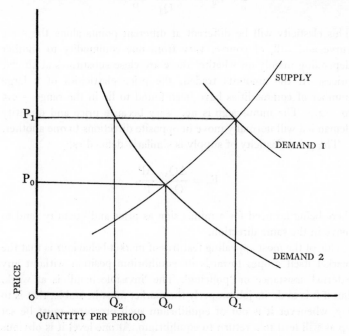

Fig. 1. Supply and Demand

5

that in every market period (a day, a week, a year) more units of the commodity would be demanded the lower its price. A demand schedule can therefore be drawn. Similarly it is assumed that in each period more units of the commodity would be offered for sale the higher the ruling price; a supply schedule can then be drawn. On these suppositions there is one price, the equilibrium or market clearing price P_0 at which an equilibrium quantity Q_0 will be both supplied and demanded.

It is useful to have a measure of the responsiveness of demand or supply to changes in price. This is given by the *price elasticity* of demand or supply. Price elasticity of demand is defined as the proportionate numerical change in amount demanded consequent upon a proportionate numerical change in price or,

$$E_d = -\frac{\Delta Q_d}{Q_d} \frac{\Delta P}{P}$$

This elasticity will be different at different points along the same curve and will, of course, vary from one commodity to another depending mainly on whether there are close substitutes at similar prices. At the amounts traded, the price elasticities of a large number of commodities have been found to lie in the range -0.5 to -2.0. The minus sign is necessary because price and quantity demanded will normally move in opposite directions to one another.

The price elasticity of supply is similarly defined as,

$$E_s = \frac{\Delta Q_s}{Q_s} \frac{\Delta P}{P},$$

there being no need for a minus sign as price and quantity tend to move in the same direction.

One of the most appealing features of market behaviour is that the market itself gropes towards its equilibrium position without any external assistance or 'policing'. The 'invisible hand' is at work. But if it is to do its job properly the market must be stable, that is to say, whenever it is out of equilibrium such pressures must be set up as will lead to a return to equilibrium. At one level it is obvious that, with the schedules as drawn, this must happen. If price is for some reason below P_0, demand will exceed supply; there will be excess demand or a sellers' market. Some people will be prepared to offer a higher price. Similarly at prices above P_0 supply will exceed demand. Suppliers will find unsold stocks on their hands and be willing to lower prices.

At a deeper level this question of adjustment for disequilibrium situations has caused economists a certain amount of bother. For one thing some actors in the market will have to take decisions about price changes. For another, there is always the possibility that response to excess supply or demand conditions will be sluggish (in which case equilibrium may never be reached) or over-enthusiastic (in which case the market might overshoot its equilibrium). This problem of adjustment is of very great importance, for without automatic and stable transition from disequilibrium situations the normative rule 'leave it to the market' loses much of its rationale.

A common source of instability is the existence of lags in supply. Supply in the current period may be a function of price in some earlier period as in the famous hog or pig cycle. Price may then move about its equilibrium in either a stable or unstable fashion. Alternatively, dealers in a market may have expectations that prices will rise, in which case they may do so even if the underlying forces of supply and demand call for constant prices.

Stable adjustment is necessary if the *laws of supply and demand* are to work. The laws will be stated here on the basis of Figure 1. Our statement is not intended to cover 'awkward' cases such as rising demand or falling supply curves. The laws of supply and demand are statements about the consequences, other things remaining unchanged, of shifts in either or both of the two schedules. Why should they shift? If people's incomes increase or their numbers grow or if they simply become fonder of a product, they will be willing to buy larger quantities at the same price, i.e., the demand curve will shift to the right.[1] Because they compare a subsequent

---

1   The science of econometrics attempts to quantify the rather loose type of qualitative statement being made in the text. A fall in price (or a rise in income) may cause people to buy more. But to find out how much more we must turn to the econometricians.

The demand schedule is drawn up on the assumption of *ceteris paribus*,

with an initial position and do not explicitly concern themselves with the process of adjustment, the laws are said to be laws of *comparative statics*. They are set out below. Only the first of these is illustrated in Figure 1 and the reader is invited to draw diagrams for the other three.

(1) An increase in demand, *ceteris paribus*, leads to an increase in price and/or quantity (to P_1 and Q_1 in the figure).

---

i.e., variables other than price (like income, population and the prices of other goods) are assumed to be known and constant. Price changes imply a movement along the curve whereas changes in these other variables imply a shift of the whole curve. A demand function or equation must include all the important variables. A commonly used equation is of the general form,

$$Q_d = A . Y^a . P^b . N^c .$$
or $$\log Q_d = \log A + a . \log Y + b . \log P + c . \log N.$$
where, Q_d is quantity demanded per period.
      A,c are constants
      Y is income
      P is price
      N is population
'a' is a coefficient measuring the income elasticity of demand,
'b' is a coefficient measuring the price elasticity of demand.

The reader is asked to recall the definition of price elasticity of demand. It should be intuitively clear that since the data are expressed in logarithms the coefficient 'b' must measure the proportionate change in quantity brought about by a proportionate change in price. Similarly, 'a' measures the income elasticity of demand (not defined in the text).

Normally the sign of 'b' is negative. A very rare case in which it is positive is known as the *Giffen good* case. But the sign of 'a' may be positive or negative. The amount demanded of most types of goods will increase with income, but for some goods it will not (poor housing, very cheap foods). Goods for which the demand falls as income increases are referred to as *inferior goods*.

In some ways the picture of the world conveyed by the equation is an excessively simplified one. It assumes explicitly that elasticities are constant along the whole curve and implicitly that the prices and quantities observed are equilibrium ones. It excludes factors which one would expect to have some influence on demand—credit rationing, expectations and stocks of assets. More complex formulations try to take some of these difficulties into account.

(2) A decrease in demand, *ceteris paribus*, leads to a decrease in price and/or quantity.

(3) An increase in supply, *ceteris paribus*, leads to a decrease in price and/or an increase in quantity.

(4) A decrease in supply, *ceteris paribus*, leads to an increase in price and/or a decrease in quantity.

The extent to which the burden of adjustment is taken up by price or by quantity depends on the elasticities of supply and demand. Consider the private housing market. Suppose that the number of households in an area increases sharply: there is a shift in the local demand schedule for housing. Law (1) states that there will be an increase in price and/or quantity. In the short term both supply and demand elasticities are likely to be low: only a small amount of extra accommodation will come forward for renting and heads of house-holds will have to take what they can get. Rents are likely to rise sharply. In the longer term both supply and demand will be more elastic. People move to lower quality accommodation or share. Existing houses are subdivided. Builders find it worthwhile to erect more houses for owner occupation. Thus rents will tend to come down from their short-term peak.

Again, suppose the costs of operating garages to rise. The elasticity condition says that if demand is inelastic (car owners do not react strongly to price increases), much of the cost increase can be passed on to the customer and there will be hardly any drop in the volume of trade. But if demand is highly elastic, very little of the cost increase will be passed on and trade will fall quite a lot.

Some prices are rigid; they do not (or are not allowed to) respond to changes in market conditions. House rents in most of western Europe are commonly fixed below market equilibrium levels. Wages tend to be rigid in a downward direction. Prices of many manufactured goods are 'administered', that is to say, set on a long-term basis with little or no regard for short-term variations in supply and demand. The main burden of adjustment is then taken up by changes in quantity.

The policy of 'leaving it to the market' implies that market equilibrium is itself desirable. The rationale for believing this to be so is considered in Chapter 4. So far, some provisional conclusions can be stated:

(1) 'Leaving it to the market' implies that a unique and stable equilibrium exists.
(2) If this is so, the laws of supply and demand will operate.
(3) The relative rôles of price and quantity change depend on the extent of price rigidity and on the sizes and variation over time of supply and demand elasticities.

The various markets

The description of markets just given was in terms of commodities or products. But there are five main types of market in which firms and households may come together as suppliers and demanders.

1. PURE EXCHANGE

Households exchange goods and services with one another, perhaps using money, perhaps not. This covers relatively trivial items (curious and jumble) but also the very important second-hand markets in cars, furniture and houses. Such transactions may dominate in poor countries. Prices, or implied prices, will be determined by haggling and by the supply and demand position. Note that this category is not limited to barter.

2. FACTOR SERVICES MARKETS

Households enter this market as suppliers of factor services thus earning incomes. Firms demand factor services and the forces of supply and demand interact to determine an equilibrium set of *hire prices*: wage rates per period of time for labour, rents for the use of land, quasi-rents for the use of buildings and machinery.

To show why the demand schedule for factor services must slope downwards it is necessary to introduce the concept *marginal physical product*. This is the addition to total output that can be made by using one extra unit of a factor service. Thus if the use of one extra unit gives an extra ten tons of output per period, the marginal physical product at that level of usage is ten tons. If this output brings in extra revenue at the rate of £2 per ton, its *marginal value product* is said to be £20. If the factor hire price is less than £20 it will be profitable for the firm concerned to take on the extra unit. If it is also the case that its marginal physical product diminishes as more of a factor service is used, it is fairly obvious that an individual firm will maximise its profit by taking on extra units up to the point at which the hire price is equal to the marginal value product (or MVP). The same will be true for all firms.

On the demand side the equilibrium condition is therefore

$$P_f = MVP.$$

The curve of marginal value product acts as the firm's demand schedule for the factor service. Its demand can be said to depend upon three things:

(1) The marginal physical productivity of the factor service,
(2) The addition to revenue consequent upon increased output,
(3) The hire price per unit of factor service.

Even under more complex circumstances (bargaining behaviour) the marginal value product of a factor still has a bearing on the hire-price obtainable for it. That is to say, if a union is bargaining on behalf of a group of people with a low marginal value product it will find itself in a weak position.

What determines the supply of factor services by households? As most households are in a position only to supply labour services we shall concentrate at first simply on these. The analysis is almost tautological. Let each household attach its own subjective valuation to each unit of factor service which it supplies and let this valuation be carried out in money terms. In the case of labour it is reasonable to assume that the value attached at the margin will rise, both because of the extra effort involved and because of competing demands on the worker's time (especially leisure). Extra factor services will be supplied up to the point at which the subjective valuation or marginal supply price (MSP) equals the hire price. Thus,

$$P_f = MSP.$$

Does the same condition hold for the services of machinery, buildings and land? It is more realistic, at a first approximation, to regard the quantities of these coming forward as fixed in the aggregate. Owners of machines will be willing, if they cannot do better, to hire them out at any price that covers maintenance; below this the machines will be scrapped.

3. FINAL GOODS MARKETS

It is impossible to show *a priori* that an individual's demand schedule for a product must be downward sloping. But it is reasonable to assume that, for most goods, negative income effects are weak. Let us assume that, just as on the factor supply side, the individual is able subjectively to value increases in the amount of each commodity available to him. Let this valuation for increments of the commodity be his marginal demand price (MDP). A downward sloping curve implies a diminishing marginal demand price. Thus the condition for the consumer to be in equilibrium is that he buys goods up to the point at which the price of the goods equals the (falling) marginal demand price,

$$P_g = MDP.$$

On the supply side, things are slightly more complicated. Under competitive conditions there will generally be a close relationship between price and marginal cost of production. *Marginal cost* is defined as the increase in total cost consequent upon the production of one more unit per period. In the short term the relationship is pretty straightforward. It can be assumed that, as plant, etc., will be fixed in the short term, the marginal cost of production will tend eventually to increase as output increases. If it pays the firm to produce at all, it will be worthwhile to produce up to that level of output at which marginal cost has risen so as to equal the going market price. At this level of output it will be maximising its profits. In the longer term, individual firms will have altered the scale of their plant either by investment in a new plant or failure to keep the existing plant intact, and firms will have had time to enter the industry or to quit it. It will still pay firms to produce an output at which price equals marginal cost, but now it will be marginal cost in a longer term sense.

Thus,
$$P_g = MC.$$

PRICES AND MARKETS

This relationship between price and marginal cost is of fundamental importance to welfare propositions based on competitive equilibrium and much use will be made of it in the next part of this book. In particular the link between long run and short run marginal cost will be more fully explored in Chapter 8.

There is a whole range of market structures, each exhibiting a different relationship between price and marginal cost (oligopoly, duopoly, monopolistic competition, cartels and various bastard forms). I do not propose to examine these in any detail. It is perhaps worth pointing out that under simple monopoly conditions (a single seller) there is a fairly precise relationship between price and marginal cost governed by the price elasticity of demand. The less the elasticity of demand the greater the producer's monopoly power and the greater the excess of price over marginal cost. Or in symbols,

$$P_g = MC \cdot \frac{e}{e-1}.\text{[1]}$$

Our main concern, however, is with the correspondence between price and marginal cost under competitive conditions.

4. INTERMEDIATE GOODS MARKETS

Much of gross output is 'used up' within the productive system and does not emerge directly in the shape of final goods—materials of all kinds, raw and semi-finished goods, and machinery. Thus steel and rolling mills are 'consumed' only indirectly, the demand for them being derived from the demand for final goods. The direct supply and demand mechanism (in the case of intermediate goods) works entirely as between firms and prices will be established as in the case of final goods. Firms will substitute between the various types of intermediate goods depending on the prices at which they are available. These flows of goods between firms are of great importance to any detailed plan for the allocation of resources. One simple way of dealing with flows of intermediate goods is by the technique of input-output analysis described in Chapter 13.

---

[1] For a proof see, for example, J. M. Henderson and R. E. Quandt, *Microeconomic Theory*, London, 1958, p. 168.

MARKETS

5. LOANS MARKET

The questions raised by this market are among the most complex in economic theory. In particular, questions of microeconomic policy cannot be considered alone; the rate of interest is inextricably bound up with the question of macroeconomic and financial policy.

First consider the relationship between interest rates and the overall level of economic activity. At low interest rates (it is alleged) businessmen will be willing to undertake more investment than at high rates. But an increase in investment expenditure raises the level of total income and at higher levels of income people will be prepared to save more. One cannot draw up demand and supply schedules for loans (or loanable funds) independently of what is happening to the overall level of income. Secondly the way in which any individual is willing to hold the assets he possesses (his 'portfolio') depends on the structure of interest rates. Some assets are very 'liquid' but carry low or zero rates of interest (like money) whereas others are less liquid but carry fairly high rates of interest (like loans to firms). In equilibrium each individual will be willing to continue holding his current portfolio at the going set of interest rates. Any change in the amount of assets to be held (including money) will cause rates of interest to alter.

I wish to push both these sets of considerations to one side. The loan market can then be characterised as follows.

The principal demand for loans will be from firms who wish to undertake new investment (to increase their stock of buildings, machines, etc.) and who wish to borrow from other firms and from households in anticipation of future profits. What is the nature of the firm's demand curve for loanable funds? The profitability of carrying out a piece of extra investment can frequently be reduced to a single rate of return expressed as a simple percentage. This rate is widely known as the *internal rate of return*.[1] Firms will carry out extra investment up to the point at which the internal rate of return is equal to the rate of interest they have to pay on loans. Clearly at low rates of interest they can be expected to carry out

---

1   That rate of discount which equates the stream of receipts and the stream of costs. For a fuller discussion see Chapter 3.

more investment than at high rates. The demand schedule for loanable funds is, then, assumed to be downward sloping. Using R to represent the internal rate of return and i to represent the going rate of interest we have

$$R = i.$$

Households will normally have a choice between present and future consumption of final goods. In the real world this choice is rather limited; it depends on hire purchase facilities, mortgage institutions and bank policies. But in a perfect capital market consumers would be able to borrow and lend at the going rate of interest. The individual will usually have a positive *rate of time preference*, that is he will prefer to have his consumption now rather than later. He will have to be offered some inducement voluntarily to forego current consumption. The extent of the subjective superiority of present goods over future goods can be expressed at the margin as a discount or interest rate. If this rate of time preference is greater than the rate of interest the individual can improve the allocation of his income over time by borrowing. (If I attach 10% more importance to income now than to income one year hence and the rate of interest is only 5%, I will try to borrow.) If my rate of time preference at the margin (MRTP) is equal to the rate of interest I will plan neither to borrow nor lend. If it is less than the rate of interest I can improve my position by lending. Each individual will, under these assumptions, adjust his saving and lending plan until

$$MRTP = i.$$

As the rate of interest rises savers will tend to save more, borrowers to borrow less and some consumers switch over from being borrowers to being lenders. The reader is warned that this analysis is essentially a full employment one. For the importance of looking at macro-economics when questions of policy are being considered, see the final sections of Chapter 5.

I have now briefly considered several main types of market. In each the individual firms and households have been assumed to adjust their behaviour in a way that is somehow optimal from their own points of view. The outcome of their behaviour is a set of 'prices' (including wage rates and interest rates) and equilibrium quantities. The whole system is a system of *general economic equilibrium*. Let us break into the system arbitrarily at some point to see how it works.

(1) Suppose that the prices of final goods are given in that they are inherited from last week or last year.

(2) At these prices firms will decide how much of each good to produce.

(3) Simultaneously they will decide how much of each factor service to use.

(4) Together with the supply curves of factor services this determines the set of factor hire-prices and the interest rate.

(5) The set of hire-prices and the ownership of resources will between them determine incomes of individuals.

(6) Incomes determine demand curves for final goods which, together with the supply curves, determine their prices.

Now the prices generated in (6) may or may not be equal to the prices initially given in (1). If they are not, the initial prices could not be today's equilibrium prices, and in a stable system of markets the process will continue until a general equilibrium has been reached.

A general equilibrium system may be characterised more simply as follows:

Given	*To be determined*
Resources and their ownership	Prices and quantities of
Preferences	all goods and services
Technical conditions	

The system is 'solved' in practice by the forces of supply and demand operating in various markets. Our description of such a system is very 'market orientated'. As we shall see in Chapter 13, it is quite possible to set out a general equilibrium model with no explicit reference to prices and markets.

Maximisation

Householders and firms have been described as though they were constantly trying to solve problems of 'constrained maximisation'. Economists make such wide use of constrained maximisation techniques that it is as well to understand the basic notion. The actor is assumed to wish to maximise or minimise something (the objective function) subject to a number of limitations (constraints). The typical consumer will not be able to have whatever he wishes, among his constraints are the disposable income available to him and the prices ruling in the market. The typical firm will find itself constrained by technical conditions of production and the resources available to it. But these do not rule out choice, subject to them the actors concerned (consumers or firms) do the best they can for themselves.

The opposite, though technically very similar, case is that of constrained minimisation. Cost minimisation is the most common instance of this. The constraint is that certain sets of output are to be produced under certain technical conditions. Subject to this constraint the managers of the firm select that method of production which will minimise costs.

What are the objective functions for firms and consumers? As far as consumers go the really important assumption from the welfare standpoint is that their behaviour should systematically reflect their preferences. The assumption inherited from hedonistic psychology was that people try to maximise *utility*. It so happens that for the rather limited purposes of demand theory this assumption is redundant (though it remains highly useful for the analysis of choice under conditions of uncertainty). Historically, economists abandoned cardinal utility in favour of ordinal utility, and ordinal utility in favour of simple axioms about choice.[1] The point of using

---

1   The assumption of cardinal utility is that a definite number of units of utility (satisfaction, pleasure) can be assigned to each bundle of goods. The assumption of ordinal utility is that bundles of goods can be ranked in order of preference (including the possibility of ties). The assumption of

these various assumptions is to establish the proposition that when price falls the quantity demanded will (other things being equal) increase—but that it may not! The case where it does not is a rather special one and has deliberately been ignored so far.

I shall be content here with a brief explanation. The effect of a fall in price may be divided up into two parts, an *income effect* and a *substitution effect*. Other things being equal, a fall in the price of a single commodity means that an individual's real income will have gone up. He may make use of this higher real income in several ways. The normal case is that he will chose to buy more of the good whose price has fallen and, indeed, of most other goods. But we cannot be absolutely sure that the income effect will be normal in this way. It may be that the good is an inferior good, that is, one of which less is bought when income increases. Whether this is the case is an empirical not an *a priori* question, and it remains true that the income effect could, in principle, go either way. The substitution effect is more reliable. Even if real income had stayed the same, the individual would wish to substitute in favour of the now cheaper commodity. Now it could happen that if the good were *very* inferior a perverse income effect might swamp the 'normal' substitution effect, the net effect being that less would be bought. This is why one has to say that the demand curve slopes downwards, but that it may not!

This perverse effect is mainly of potential importance not in the final goods markets but rather in the factor services and loans markets. An income tax may cause some individuals to offer more

---

revealed preference is concerned only with actually observed behaviour. The axioms of revealed preference are that:

(a) More goods will be chosen rather than less whenever the choice exists.
(b) Bundles previously rejected will not be chosen when those previously chosen are still available. This may be put in either a *weak* form in which ties are allowed, or in a *strong* form in which they are not and is known as the *consistency* condition.
(c) If bundle A is chosen rather than bundle B, and bundle B is chosen rather than bundle C, bundle C will not be chosen rather than bundle A. This is the *transitivity* condition.

labour, not less, so that the supply curve of labour services is backward sloping at least over a range. Similarly, a rise in the rate of interest may cause some people to save less, not more. The most plausible case would be where an individual was saving for a particular sum at a given future date. In the general explanation of markets I have been assuming that awkward cases of this kind do not occur. Where they do occur it is possible that more than one market equilibrium exists and that some of these will be unstable.

Returning to the main point, the aim of the consumer is taken to be a desire to reach a preferred position, but it is very convenient indeed to talk *as though* he were trying to maximise (ordinal) utility. Using the simple framework of constrained maximisation, some powerful generalisations are possible. Consider an individual's consumption and expenditure plan for a number of periods ahead. In each period he must decide how much work and of which types to undertake. Current consumption of goods has to be traded, as it were, against leisure. But current consumption has also to be traded against future consumption; that is, within the utility maximising framework the consumer must decide on how much borrowing or how much lending to do. These are not arbitrary decisions; they must (if any normative juice is to be squeezed out of the competitive stone) be the conscious outcome of a subjective maximising process.

The corresponding assumption to utility maximisation on the business side is that firms try to maximise profits. Simple propositions such as

$$P_g = MC \quad \text{and} \quad P_f = MVP$$

depend crucially on this assumption. Paradoxically the profit maximisation assumption is by no means self-evidently true. It may or may not be in the interests of salaried managers to pursue profit at the expense of other goals (see Chapter 14). But in perfectly competitive conditions the single firm is forced to maximise profits or to go out of business so long as competing firms try to do so. Profits are to be maximised subject to the ruling prices of goods and factor services and to the conditions of production. Technical conditions of production can, in principle, be described in terms of production functions, i.e., equations or sets of equations linking together bundles of outputs and efficiently used bundles of inputs. A lot of methods of production will be quite obviously hopeless: they will be dominated by alternative methods which use less of all inputs. Among those which are not so dominated, the manager will be able to apply the *principle of substitution*. He will substitute in favour of those factor services which become relatively cheap.

Various types of production function are possible. The traditional competitive model is based on one in which any bundle of outputs may be produced by any one of a large number of different processes, each making rather different use of the various inputs available.[1] Any change in input prices will mean that a new process is selected (for the former process ceases to be the least-cost one). I shall use the term 'neo-classical' to describe production functions in which continuous substitutability is possible, though historically the term requires constant returns to scale as well. A different (and linear) production function is described in Chapter 11.

Summary

In the hypothetical competitive model the quantities of goods to be produced and factor services to be used are determined in a

---

1   A simple form of production function in which continuous substitution is possible is the Cobb-Douglas function which may be written,

$$Q = A. L.^{\alpha} K.^{\beta}$$

where   Q is quantity produced per period

A is a constant

L is labour services (man hours)

K is machine hours

α is a coefficient measuring the elasticity of response of output to labour services

β is a coefficient measuring the elasticity of response of output to machine services.

These two coefficients perform the same rôle on the supply side as did the coefficients 'a' and 'b' on the demand side. They show the proportionate change in output consequent upon a proportionate change in the amount of input used. The reader is left to write out the formulation in logarithms. One or two technical aspects of α and β may be noted (but not proved). There are decreasing, constant or increasing returns to scale depending on whether the sum of the two coefficients, $\alpha + \beta$, is less than, equal to, or

PRICES AND MARKETS

decentralised fashion within a general system of markets. Prices in these markets are beyond the control of individual actors (firms and households) who, nevertheless, faced with these prices, act in an optimising way. The task now is to see whether this system is in any sense optimal. Is competitive equilibrium a good thing? As a preliminary to this we must look a little more closely at the rôle of time and interest rates.

---

greater than unity. Further, under competitive conditions, α is the share of total output going to labour and β the share of output going to the owners of machines. Attempts to fit this type of equation to empirical data are fraught with difficulty and their interpretation, when fitted, is a matter of controversy. Nevertheless there has been a large number of studies both at the micro and macroeconomic levels. At the level of individual firms, studies have suggested a situation of near constant returns in the mass of manufacturing industries and of slightly increasing returns in a few of them. At the national level controversy has centred around the percentage of output growth apparently associated with general economic advance rather than increases in labour and plant as such (see R. Solow, 'Technical Progress and Productivity Change', *Review of Economics and Statistics*, vol. 39, 1957 and D. Jorgenson and Z. Griliches, 'Explanation of Productivity Change', *Review of Economic Studies*, vol. 34, 1967. Both of these are reprinted in A. K. Sen (ed.), *Growth Economics*, London, 1970).

Notice that increasing or constant returns do not contradict our previous assumption of diminishing marginal physical products. The latter relates to increases in the amount of one factor service, the others remaining unchanged. The former relates to increases in all identifiable factors taken together.

3 TIME

At several points in the rest of this book it will be useful to refer to the concept of net present value and the process of 'time discounting'. It is, for example, quite impossible to discuss big business or public enterprise or economic welfare without an adequate treatment of *time*. A short introduction is therefore provided in this chapter.

The planning period

I shall assume that each firm, household or planner makes decisions relevant to a planning period that stretches from the present moment as far as the planning horizon at which lies the terminal date of the plan. There is no objective way of knowing how long the planning period should be. Use of the concept does *not* imply that the planner has no interest in what happens after the terminal date. He is free to plan that his assets (his terminal assets) will be of such and such a size at the terminal date. The bigger these are, the stronger his interest in the post-horizon future.

Present value

Decision-makers will *not* be indifferent as to the date on which payments have to be made or on which receipts are due. The two sets of reasons for this have already been indicated in Chapter 2. For various reasons (some of them often alleged to be 'irrational') people will have positive rates of time preference, that is to say they will prefer to receive a given sum of money sooner rather than later. If they are asked to postpone current consumption they will ask for more consumption at a later date. In terms of our present institutions they will demand interest. The other set of reasons has to do with productivity. Income postponed could have been used by the individual for undertaking some act of investment during the intervening period.

For these two sets of reasons, people will attach higher values to money flows the earlier they are expected to occur. A simple technical device for taking this into account is to convert the stream of dated sums of money to a *present value* by multiplying them by a *discount factor*. The discount factor is given by

$$D = \frac{1}{(1 + i)^t}$$

where i is the rate of interest or discount thought appropriate by the decision maker and t is the 'date' of the money flow. Suppose the discount rate to be 5%, then £21 to be received next year has a present value of only £20. Had the discount rate been 10% the present value would have been about £19. Two things should be noticed:

(1) With a given discount rate the present value gets smaller the more distant the expected money flow, i.e., the distant future is less important than the near future;

(2) the present value of a given stream of expected money flows, is less the greater the rate of discount.

For actual calculations the discount factor can, of course, be derived very easily from a standard set of discount tables. Contrary to the belief of some enthusiastic practitioners the device is a very old one, long known to economists and accountants.

Stocks and flows

I have already distinguished between factors of production (which are a stock concept) and factor services (a flow concept). In the various markets described in Chapter 2, the prices of factor services are determined, not the prices of factors themselves. The discounting procedure just described is a simple way of linking the valuation of stocks and flows.

Consider four examples. In the theory of the firm to be used in Chapter 14, the value of a firm is given from the present value of the stream of future profits it is expected to earn. It would be worth paying this sum of money (but no more) in order to acquire the firm.

Secondly consider a piece of land. Various uses will be possible; for each there will be an expected stream of receipts and costs. The more lucrative the use the greater the present value and the higher the price at which it will be exchanged. It is for this reason that economists since Ricardo have taught that the rent of land is 'price-determined not price-determining'. It is not the high price of land that makes office blocks expensive but the profitability of office blocks that keeps land prices high. (For everyday transactions in land the discounting procedure is not, in fact, much used. Valuers tend to work with the much rougher rule-of-thumb that land will exchange at x year's purchase. This is a permissible short-cut when values are generally stable and interest rates stay much the same; otherwise it is only a crude approximation.) Thirdly, consider human beings. As economic units their present value is the discounted sum of all the future income they are expected to produce, i.e., of their labour services. On this view people can be considered as making up a stock of *human capital* which can be improved by, for example, education. Fourthly consider a machine. Once again its present value is the discounted sum of the stream of profits to be earned by employing it.

Investment criteria

An investment project can usually be written down as a series of monetary inflows and outflows (benefits and costs) expected over a number of years. Characteristically, there will be a major payment at the beginning of the project (the purchase of factory buildings, machines, etc.), a series of net receipts over its useful life and perhaps a small receipt for scrap value at the very end. The criterion referred to most frequently in this book is the net present value (NPV) criterion. This states that a project is acceptable if

Present value of receipts
—present value of operating and maintenance costs $\Big\}$ exceeds zero
—initial outlay

or

$$NPV > 0$$

A closely related criterion uses the 'internal rate of return' or 'marginal productivity of investment'. This is a little bit more difficult to explain. We have already noticed that NPV falls as the rate of discount increases. There must therefore be some point at which NPV crosses over from being positive to negative. The rate of discount at which this crossing over occurs is defined as the internal rate of return. If the rate of return R exceeds the rate of interest or discount (i) the project is acceptable. Thus

$$R > i$$

is the appropriate criterion.

For complex projects these two criteria can yield different results but for a wide range of real world decisions they are inter-changeable. Difficulties certainly arise when two or more projects have to be compared with one another and have differing lengths of life or different capital outlays. In the first case it is necessary to make assumptions about what happens to funds in the period between the end of the shorter project and the end of the longer one and, in the second case, about how (if at all) the funds 'left-over' would be used were the smaller project adopted.

Figure 2 shows the effect on the net present value of a hypothetical investment project of altering the discount rate. The internal rate of return is 8%. Suppose the discount rate to be 4%; the project would be clearly acceptable as NPV exceeds zero and 8% exceeds 4%.

The use of NPV is quite common in industry under the general heading of DCF or 'discounted cash flow'. The technique itself is however quite general in that it can be used equally in the public or private sector and in profit and non-profit seeking enterprises.

Switching

A change in the discount rate will have important real effects on the composition and the time pattern of investment as well as on its total. It is useful to have the term *capital intensive* for projects whose outgoings are bunched at a relatively early stage in the life of a project or its receipts bunched at a relatively late stage. Capital intensive projects are likely to do badly when discount rates rise, for the powerful arithmetic of compound interest ensures that the

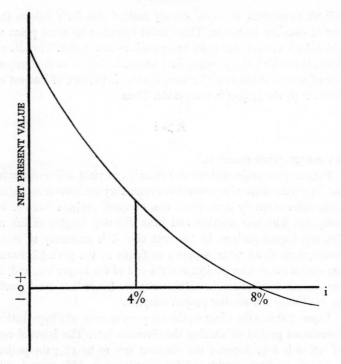

Fig. 2. Discount Rates and Net Present Value

present value of costs will not fall much while the present value of receipts will fall a great deal. Thus two projects could switch over (their ranking could be reversed) as a result of a change in the discount rate. It is important that planners should be aware of this effect. Discount rates may rise for short term balance of payments reasons. Consequent effects on the composition of investment might be wholly unintended. A run on the pound could cause conventional power stations to be adopted instead of nuclear ones! One would need to be satisfied that high discount rates really did reflect a shortage of capital.

A numerical example of the sort of switchover I have in mind is given in the following table.

	Year 0	Year 1	Year 2	Net Present Value @10%	@20%
Project A	−150	+200	+50	+74	+51
Project B	−150	+30	+250	+85	+48

The table gives the net present values of two projects A and B at the two rates of discount 10% and 20%. Initial outlay is the same in each case and both projects finish at the end of year 2. But project B is more 'capital intensive'; it is therefore likely to come off relatively badly at high rates of discount. The ranking of the two projects is reversed as a result of a change in the discount rate.[1]

The reader is invited to graph the figures in the table in the same manner as in Figure 2. What is the rate of discount at which the two projects switch over?

Uncertainty

I have been careful to talk in terms of 'expected' receipts and costs. One can never be certain about the future. There are various techniques for taking uncertainty into account, none of them fully satisfactory. One should not be misled by the employment of some impressive technical device into believing that uncertainty has somehow been eliminated. The most obvious and in some ways the best device is to present several outcomes on an 'optimistic', 'normal', 'pessimistic' basis and leave the decision maker to make his own guess about an uncertain future. Sometimes, though rarely, it is possible to make use of probabilities as in the water resource example of Chapter 9. Apparently simple devices (like using a higher rate of

---

1   One should note that 're-switching' is a possibility. The nature of the two projects A and B may be such that while a fall in the rate of interest from 20% to 10% causes A to be chosen rather than B, a further fall in the interest rate would cause a re-switching to B.

discount) are almost always misleading. The most interesting situations are those in which people have to choose between a moderately profitable but fairly certain project and a highly profitable but very uncertain project. The final decision in this type of case really does rest with the 'decision-maker'; the economist has done his job by setting out the possibilities.

Social rate of discount

It is widely alleged that people will privately have rates of time preference that are too high from the social point of view; they have a defective telescopic faculty, they are too myopic. Further, it is alleged that they would, by collective agreement, be willing to forego more consumption in the knowledge that others were making similar sacrifices. If this line of argument is accepted, the total amount of investment will be too low if left to private individuals and the state must take a hand. A contrary argument is that in any case future generations will be better off than we are, due to the steady pace of technological progress. Why should I be expected to transfer some of my consumption to the next (richer) generation?

This type of debate tends to be inconclusive; it comes down in the end to the issue of consumers' sovereignty. There is no special reason why a government should regard the decisions thrown up by the free market as sacrosanct. If planners believe that the market's rate of time preference is too high they can react in several possible ways. The most extreme type of reaction is to impose forced saving during a process of rapid industrialisation as was done under Stalin from the beginning of the first five year plan. It is useful to think of the Stalin policy as maximising the stock of capital equipment at some future date (the end year of the plan) subject to the need for a certain minimum of consumer goods for each year of the intervening period.

Another possibility, in a mixed economy, is to use a lower rate of time preference within the public sector. This would lead to an increase in the volume of public investment as managers would be allowed to use a lower rate of discount. If one takes seriously the 'efficiency' type of argument to be used in the next chapter, one should not use different discount rates in different sectors. 'Too much' investment would take place in that sector with the lower discount rate. Further, a low discount rate in the public sector would not only cause its managers to do more investment but also make them favour more capital-intensive projects. And this may not be at all what was intended. On the whole, public sector investment projects can be justified by virtue of the costs and benefits themselves (including externalities, which are fully treated in Chapter 7) not merely by the use of a lower discount rate.

To say that society should use a lower rate of discount than the market would use, if left to its own devices, is to say that investment should be greater than it would be in free market conditions. The important point for us at present is that this is a clear question of *social choice*. The choice of the path of consumption over time *is* a question of making value judgements; to 'leave it to the market' is itself to make one. The more interesting question is whether the market, society having made its judgement, can be used as a device for decentralising particular investment decisions.

4 WELFARE

The core of this chapter is a simple theorem about competitive equilibrium: *that every competitive equilibrium is a Pareto-optimum.* One or two definitions are needed.

(A) A potential improvement. This is a change (probably as a result of some policy measure) such that it *would be possible* for those who gain to compensate those who lose and still be better off themselves. Ignoring awkward cases,[1] this implies an increase in an index number representing real income. It is presumably true that almost all acts of economic policy (except for overtly redistributive ones) are intended to be potential improvements.

(B) An actual improvement. This is a change such that some people *are* made better off without others being made worse off. A potential improvement can be converted into an actual improvement by the payment of compensation.

Consider a reduction in tariffs on imported goods or a reduction in cotton textile quotas. Under certain circumstances it will happen that resources move out of previously sheltered trades to sectors in which their marginal value products are now higher. If this is so there will have been an increase in real income or a potential improvement; consumers in general could more than compensate those people who have had to change their occupations. But it will remain a potential improvement unless compensation really does take place. Consider next the building of an urban motorway. If the value of time saved, etc., exceeds the costs of the motorway (including the 'costs' of such things as noise disturbance) its construction will constitute a potential improvement or an increase in real income. But only if all those people who suffer in some way are *in fact* compensated will there be an actual improvement.

The notion underlying the basic theorem stated above is that in a

---

1   These can occur, in principle, when the above test of a real income increase holds but when it is also the case, that potential losers could bribe potential gainers to maintain the status quo! I shall assume that such cases are of little practical importance.

freely operating market only actual improvements will be adopted. Making an actual improvement can be defined, after the Italian economist Pareto, as moving to a Pareto-better situation.

(C) A Pareto-optimum. This is a state of the system such that all Pareto-better moves have been exhausted; no one can now be made better off without somebody else being made worse off. The competitive system discards all outcomes which are not Pareto-optimal; in this sense it is efficient.

The efficiency of competition

I now reconsider the various markets already examined and show (without formal proof) how Pareto-optimality will come about as a result of the competitive process. The easiest method is to set out whole strings of marginal equivalences where price is in each the linking factor.

1. EXCHANGE

The analysis is almost tautological but essential to the rest of the argument. Two people would not enter into an exchange arrangement unless they each expected to gain by it. Contrast this with the medieval notion that one party always gained at the expense of another during the process of trade and with what happens when one party is in a monopoly position. This simple analysis of mutual benefit is, by the way, the defence for freedom of contract.

2. FACTOR SERVICES

The analysis is provided here for one factor service only but can easily be extended to any number of factor services. If its marginal value product differed between occupations it would be possible to reallocate it so as to increase the value of total output, i.e., by moving units from those firms in which their marginal product is low to those where it is high. But under competitive conditions we have seen that each firm will hire units of a factor service up to the point at which its price (e.g., its wage rate) equals its marginal value product and that the price facing each firm will be the same. Hence, under competition, marginal value products will be equal everywhere,

$$MVP_1 = MVP_2$$

where 1 and 2 represent any two goods in which the factor is used. Thus, at the ruling prices of goods, the total value of output is maximised as an outcome of the behaviour of individual profit maximising firms. But we have already seen that, once output is determined, the outcome of exchange will be Pareto-optimal. A movement from a disequilibrium to an equilibrium position in the factor services markets is a condition for overall efficiency.

On the factor service supply side, if marginal supply price differed as between households it would be 'efficient' to adjust the supply of factor services such that households with high marginal supply prices offered less and those with low marginal supply prices offered more. But under competition, price (e.g., wage-rate) equals marginal supply price. Hence

$$MSP_1 = MSP_2$$

where 1 and 2 are any two households supplying the factor service. No further improvement is possible once competitive equilibrium is reached.

From these two equations it can readily be seen that in competitive equilibrium the value attached to the marginal unit of a factor service by firms is equal to the value attached to it by the households which supply it, i.e.

$$MVP = P_f = MSP.$$

3. FINAL GOODS

In competitive equilibrium the price of a commodity is equal to its marginal cost of production (see Chapter 2). As the price facing each firm is the same, marginal cost will tend to be the same at each firm's equilibrium level of output. Thus, in a disequilibrium situation, output will be reallocated among firms, those with low marginal costs producing more and those with high marginal costs less. This ensures that the total cost of producing the good is minimised.

$$MC_1 = MC_2$$

where 1 and 2 are two firms producing the good under consideration. If factor services are in some sense correctly priced, a movement from a disequilibrium to an equilibrium allocation of output as between firms will make it possible to produce more of some goods without producing less of others, i.e., it will lead to efficiency in production.

Can something similar be said on the demand side? Each consumer is in equilibrium at a point where price equals marginal demand price. But price is the same for everybody. Hence marginal demand price is the same for everybody. It follows that the total value attached to a good, say bread, is maximised by taking it away from people who, at the margin, value it a little and giving it to people who value it a lot. This is precisely what the market achieves!

$$MDP_1 = MDP_2$$

where 1 and 2 are two households consuming the good under discussion.

Notice that this condition for efficiency is perfectly consistent with a society some of whose members are grossly overfed and others grossly undernourished. Competition equates the *money* amounts people are prepared to offer at the margin. If they have very little money this in no way affects the 'efficiency' characteristics of competitive equilibrium. Obviously this is a very important matter and we return to it shortly.

Meanwhile it will be true that the marginal demand price attached to the good by any one consumer equals the marginal cost to any one firm or

$$MDP = P_g = MC[1].$$

4. INTERMEDIATE GOODS

Many intermediate goods are 'produced means of production'. They are produced by firms for other firms and do not directly

---

1   Putting some of the above relationships together and using the additional relationship that $Pg = P_f/MPP$, where MPP is marginal physical product, we have $MDP = MSP/MPP$. This is precisely the condition that would apply if a Robinson Crusoe were transforming his own factor services *directly* into goods for his own consumption.

involve the subjective valuations of households. For efficiency, any given supply of them should be used so as to maximise the total value of output produced (marginal value product should be everywhere equal) and should be produced at minimum cost (marginal cost should be equal wherever they are produced).

5. LOANS MARKET

We noted in the previous chapter that the volume of investment and the rate of interest thrown up by the market may not be optimal. The basic theorem stated at the beginning of the present chapter insists, however, that regardless of whether the decision is optimal it will nevertheless be efficient. On the demand side, the internal rate of return equals the interest rate for each firm. Hence the internal rate will be the same for all firms

$$R_1 = R_2.$$

It is therefore impossible to reallocate investment funds between firms so as to increase the total return from investment projects. On the supply side, by similar reasoning, the marginal rate of time preference will be equal for each household or

$$MRTP_1 = MRTP_2.$$

If they are not equal the subjective cost of carrying out any volume of saving may be reduced by having those households with a low rate of time preference save more and those with high rates of time preference save less. This is precisely what competition is supposed to achieve! Bringing the equations together, the marginal rate of time preference of any household is equal to the internal rate of return of any marginal project.

Notice the immensely important role played by prices. Though not important in themselves they enter the analysis as a means of enabling the strings of marginal equivalences (only a few of which I have discussed) to hold under decentralised market conditions.

The theorem that every competitive equilibrium is a Pareto-optimum provides the core of the case for 'leaving it to the market'. It is necessary to say, however, that there is another, more robust defence of the free market which we have so far ignored, a 'biological'

34

defence, as it were. The pressures of competition drive entrepreneurs constantly to search out new processes and techniques. It is the search for profit that generates technical progress and it is technical progress that generates economic growth. The difficulty with this defence is that much of the basic research in the private sector is carried out within large 'bureaucracies'. Pressures there are, but not pressures of the crude 'competitive-drive' type. We shall see in Chapter 14 that the motives of managers in a large modern corporation may be much more complicated than that.

The transition

I now want to consider the nature of the conditions necessary to convert statements like 'competitive equilibrium is efficient' to statements like 'leaving it to the market is a good thing'. There are *ethical* conditions and *technical* conditions. Two major ethical postulates can be distinguished:

(1) Individualism is a 'good thing'
(2) The distribution of income and property is just,

and are now discussed in turn.

The first postulate suggests that the preferences of individuals are all important, that any statements about the welfare of society as a whole are based on component changes in individual welfare. This postulate is very widely accepted. It denies that there is any 'common good' or 'social welfare' other than some sort of weighted sum of individual welfare. It is possible, of course, to take quite an opposite view—that individual preferences are not to count for much and that the state should set out goals for the economic system on a collectivist basis for the greater good. In order to avoid confusion with some of the technical failures of a market system it is best, for the sake of the present discussion, to leave altogether on one side questions of the irrationality of individual consumers, of their vulnerability to advertising and so on. This postulate of individualism is *not* confined to market type situations. Even if all economic decisions are to be taken centrally the question still arises of how to take heed of individual preferences (as expressed, for example, in voting behaviour).

If individuals are to count (which seems reasonable—at least for some types of good) there are certain difficulties in putting together information about individual welfare in order to derive information about social welfare. A formal statement of preferences for society as a whole is known as a *social welfare function*. Now Arrow's 'general possibility theorem'[1] states that it is impossible to move from individual preferences to social welfare without violating one of a number of conditions. It is not necessary to examine these here in detail. The conditions, at least one of which must be violated, are very plausible. For example, one of them is that social choice should not be 'dictatorial', that is the preferences of 'society' should not coincide with the preferences of any individual. The whole question of how far the state should be *paternalistic* is central to this discussion. The paternalist easily finds his way out of Arrow's impasse; he simply drops the condition that social choice should not be dictatorial. Put like this it sounds a very wicked thing to do. But all it means is that society's preferences about, say, the health service are assumed for purposes of policy making to coincide with the preferences of the Minister of Health and a handful of his colleagues. I shall return to this question of paternalism in Chapter 15.

For the present I shall simply point out that almost the whole of welfare economics takes the desirability of economic individualism for granted and that this is essentially an ethical judgement about the kind of society we want to see.

The other ethical postulate was about the distribution of income and property. To see the relevance of this to competitive equilibrium we must go back to some of the marginal conditions. It was seen that the most efficient way of allocating a given output of goods among consumers was that

$$MDP_1 = MDP_2$$

or that the subjective money valuation of output by consumers

---

1   J. K. Arrow, *Social Choice and Individual Values*, 2nd ed., New York, 1963.

would be maximised, brought about by a competitive equilibrium of exchange. But MDP is the amount that individual is actually willing to pay for an extra unit of commodity and, as a simple generalisation, he will be prepared to pay more the greater his income. Thus the optimality or desirability (as opposed to the efficiency) of the equilibrium condition depends upon the optimality or desirability of the distribution of income (and therefore property). The statement that competitive equilibrium is a 'good thing' *cannot* be neutral or 'value free'.

One may generalise this conclusion in terms of Pareto-optimality. Competitive equilibrium is Pareto-optimal and Pareto-optimality is our condition of efficiency. However, not one but a large number of Pareto-optima is possible, each corresponding to a different distribution of income and resources. This is very awkward for advocates of the free market but not insuperable. Can one accept the conclusion and still argue for the optimality of the free market?

As long as we are allowed to dichotomise (to split into two separate parts) the economy there is a simple way out. I like to call this the 'neo-classical liberal' solution. First of all one achieves whichever distribution of income is thought to be just or fair by redistributing goods and resources between individuals. This is entirely a matter of value judgement, whether the economists' or the politicians'. But having done this, one simply lets an efficient competitive equilibrium emerge, that is, the distributive and efficiency aspects are dichotomised.

The major criticism of a neo-classical liberal solution is that the economy cannot really be dichotomised in this way. Any redistribution of income comes about in practice by acts of fiscal policy. But if a unit tax (T) is imposed on, say, income from labour services the former conditions for equilibrium in the labour market are replaced by

$$MSP = P_f - T < P_f = MVP$$

i.e., marginal supply price is no longer equal to marginal value product and the new equilibrium cannot be Pareto-optimal. The very act of redistributing income itself affects the efficiency conditions. Which brings us to a short-coming of Pareto-better movements (or improvements) as a criterion of good acts of policy. I may prefer a situation in which the efficiency conditions are not met but the distribution of income is (in my opinion) just, to a Pareto-optimal situation in which the distribution of income (again in my opinion) is unjust. Being Pareto-better is not a necessary condition of a change constituting a 'good thing'.

To recapitulate, the two basic ethical postulates needed are concerned with the importance of economic individualism and with the 'justness' of the distribution of income and property.

Apart from these ethical considerations a number of technical conditions must remain unviolated. The most important of these are as follows:

(1) There must be no imperfections in factor service or product markets,

(2) There must be no increasing or constant returns in production,

(3) There must be no divergence between marginal social and private costs (benefits).

There is a further condition which has already been discussed,

(4) Disequilibrium behaviour must be such that equilibrium in single markets can be reached and markets must be inter-related in such a way as to produce a stable general equilibrium.

Insofar as actual free markets do not satisfy these rather stringent conditions they are likely to 'fail' in searching for efficient solutions to the economic problem. These departures are in the nature of technical hitches unlike the two great ethical objections about the rôle of individualism and distributive justice.

1. The first technical hitch is that neither households nor firms need be price-takers. Households (in their capacity of sellers of factor services) and firms (in their capacity of sellers of intermediate or final goods) may have some control over the prices they are able to charge. They may simply be taking advantage of favourable market conditions or they may be organised into trades unions (on the factor services side) or selling cartels (on the products side). We have already noticed that, under conditions of simple monopoly,

price will be above marginal cost of production by an amount which is greater the smaller the price elasticity of demand

$$MDP = P_g = MC \frac{e}{e + 1}.$$

Consumers are no longer choosing between goods on the basis of their marginal cost of production, and the efficiency conditions are violated.

A neo-classical liberal will wish to overcome this technical hitch by breaking up monopolies or forcing them to bring price closer to marginal cost. This type of piecemeal policy will be assessed in theoretical terms in Part II and in terms of practical application in Chapter 14.

2. The second technical hitch is that firms may experience non-decreasing returns to scale (often referred to as the problem of non-convexity).[1] It can readily be shown that increasing or constant returns and perfect competition cannot both hold at the same time. Or rather that competition under these conditions contains the seeds of its own destruction as any one firm could grow without limit until it had swallowed up the whole. If at some initial situation the ruling market price were above marginal cost and marginal cost were falling as output increased, it would always be the case that

$$P_g > MC.$$

It is important to understand why it is that increasing returns is a 'problem'. The fact that is incompatible with a highly artificial construct of economic theorists should not cause undue anxiety (after all it is very pleasing to experience increasing returns). The 'problem' arises because it is hard to draw up a simple set of decision rules (like $P_g = MC$) that will permit efficient decentralised decision taking. The difficulty is not only about perfect competition, it is about efficient decentralisation generally.

3. The third technical hitch is that marginal private cost (paid by

---

1   If there are increasing returns to scale, parts of the production possi-bility curve (see Chapter 17) will be convex to the *origin*.

the actor) may or may not be equal to marginal social cost (paid by everybody, including the initial actor), the difference being an 'externality'. In these circumstances an improvement might be obtained by interfering in such a way as to make the actor take the externality into account. Various devices for bringing this about are discussed in Chapter 7. The most dramatic examples are where marginal social costs exceed marginal private costs due to the production of some nuisance jointly with a good, for example, pollution accompanies oil transportation, noise is generated by motor vehicles. The competitive mechanism cannot be relied upon, in these circumstances, to bring about an efficient solution. The solution closest in spirit to 'leaving it to the market' is to rely upon bargaining between affected parties, or upon litigation, to make actors take into account the external effects of their actions.

The conclusion of this section is fairly clear. A competitive equilibrium is a 'good thing' if the ethical postulates and the technical conditions are met. But these are very severe stipulations. No market economy is likely to meet all of them. That is why very few economists can be found who advocate complete laissez-faire. Perhaps the classical writers came nearest to it and their attitude is discussed in the next chapter.

Politico-economic systems

Politico-economic systems can usefully be classified by the attitude taken in them to the two ethical postulates. The preferences of a society may be based on the private preferences of individuals (individualism) or upon a communal view (collectivism) or they may be mixed. There is, broadly, a right-left distinction here. Similarly the ownership of resources may be purely private or private-but-redistributed (by tax policies) or wholly public or some mixture of these. Again there is a right-left distinction.

The more extreme types of system stand out as combining extreme left (or extreme right) with regard to each ethical postulate. Thus where both the ownership of resources and preferences are entirely individually based we have a laissez-faire system and where they are entirely publicly based a purely *command* system. Various in-between cases are rather more interesting. Where preferences are private but the ownership of resources public we have a *market-socialist system*. Where preferences are private and resource ownership is private (but redistributed) we have what I would call a *radical right* system. In most systems of social democracy both preferences and resource ownership are mixed. The reader is invited to try to complete the classification.

Our distinction between ethical and technical conditions is useful here. It is often argued that the politico-economic systems of the East and the West are moving closer together. Presumably this could be taken to mean that both sets of economies were adopting central positions, that is, that in eastern European countries more stress was being put on private preferences of consumers and that in western countries the state was becoming a major owner of resources. This may be so. But very much greater similarities show themselves on the technical side (by technical, here, I mean economic control systems, not technology) where the search for efficient methods of decentralising decisions once the major policy questions have been settled, is revealing common problems. At this level the technical conditions for efficiency show a surprising robustness—right across politico-economic systems.

5 RETROSPECT

In this chapter I shall discuss the views of a few important groups of economic writers on the rôle of the free market. The possible field is vast and any reader who wishes to delve further is referred to Schumpeter's monumental work.[1]

Newcomers to the subject will find that a rough general understanding of the technical terms used is enough to get them by.

The classical free market

'Classical' writers are those (mainly British) from David Hume to John Stuart Mill who believed, broadly, that the pursuit of self-interest, hedged about by laws of property, contract and so on would lead to high levels of national income and high rates of economic progress. The policy implications of this view were the dismantling of restrictive trading regulations, free foreign trade, a free labour market and a minimal rôle for the state. Some historians of economic thought have come to refer to this, rather clumsily, as a 'market-plus-framework' ideology. Classical writers differed as to how much framework there should be but, almost unanimously, rejected outright intervention in the actual operation of markets. Much discussion of how 'interventionist' these writers actually were turns upon the semantic issue of how one defines the word 'policy'.

It is widely (and I believe correctly) held that classical writers (Ricardo, McCulloch, James Mill the elder) advocated a policy of laissez-faire. How far they managed to influence policy decisions is a question for detailed investigation rather than generalisation, but we do know that certain individual writers were of direct importance on specific issues. An essential part of the framework was a stable currency and Ricardo, partly through his influence on Peel, was very important in securing the resumption of cash payments by the

---

1   J. A. Schumpeter, *History of Economic Analysis*, London, 1963.

Bank of England in 1819. Nassau Senior drafted the New Poor Law of 1834 and the 1841 report on the handloom weavers. McCulloch was economic adviser to Melbourne's government. But on the other issues, such as the move towards freer trade, the process was less direct; pressure for lower import duties came through Ricardo's disciples by way of the Board of Trade while pressure for abolition of the Corn Laws took the form of Manchesterisn or 'vulgar' political economy. In this period as in all others, the influence of thinkers on policy was highly complex and requires political, sociological and psychological as well as economic explanations.

Robustness, rather than analytical precision, characterised the main steam of classical writing on policy. Not until the present century was a proof offered that competition would lead to economic efficiency. Most writers were content to draw an analogy between the individual's and the state's economic well-being. Thus Smith, 'what is prudence in the conduct of every private family can scarce be folly in that of a great kingdom'. But it was Smith, too, who came closest to giving a proof that competition leads to efficiency. He suggests that wage rates and rates of profit are brought into equality with one another during the process of competition. These rates act as signals that show labour and capital where they can most productively be used. The real cost of restrictions on trade was that they distorted the pattern of profit rates thus causing capital to flow into relatively unproductive uses. With somewhat less precision Smith also held that under competition the amount of savings would be such as to permit the maximum (best?) rate of capital accumulation. Thus competition would produce not only static efficiency but efficiency over time.

The *labour market* illustrates the basic policy problem rather well. A free market in labour was desirable on grounds of efficiency and the 'new political economy' advocated the abandonment of the old system of outdoor relief which was alleged to lead to high parish rates and low wages. It was accompanied by idleness, inefficient use of labour, lower rates of capital accumulation and, in the end, a lower 'wages-fund'. But a reform of the labour market could hardly fail to provide for the poor and the 1834 Act admirably combined an absolutely minimum protection for the poor with a freely operating

43

labour market. The Act abolished outdoor relief for the able-bodied, offering shelter in the notorious 'unions' on the basis of 'less eligibility'; that is, the amount of relief was such as to bring the pauper to the level of the poorest agricultural labourer (in practice, more than this had commonly to be given). This policy was not interventionist. It sought to discharge society's obligation to the poor in the way least harmful to economic development and displayed minimal sympathy with pauper families.

The basic postulate of a free labour market is that the labourer is a free agent, fully capable of entering into contracts. Children (and possibly women) were not free agents and clearly required protection. Classical writers were therefore broadly sympathetic to the regulation of factory hours up to 1833. Their sticking point was the regulation of adult labourers who, unlike women and children, could be regarded as free agents. Senior and others felt (rightly) that regulation of women's hours must necessarily lead to the regulation of males as well and strongly opposed legislation after 1833.

More dramatic (and analytically more difficult) was the problem of technological unemployment, notably the handloom weavers. One or two writers, including Barton and (in his later years) Ricardo had argued that an increase in capital accummulation could lead to a fall in the wages fund and consequently a fall in wage-rates or a rise in unemployment. If this were so, arguments for putting a tax on machinery, rejected by classical orthodoxy, would begin to look a little more respectable. Ricardo had already pointed out, however, that machinery would increase total real income and capital accumulation and that this effect must sooner or later outweight the initial reduction in the wages fund. Both McCulloch and John Stuart Mill accepted the long term effect as being the dominant one and therefore opposed any discouragement to the introduction of machinery. Similarly, Senior, using a more straightforward supply and demand analysis, successfully opposed the artificial regulation of handloom weavers' wages.

These three policy issues in the labour market illustrate that a freely operating labour market must be provided with a framework that protects those who do rather badly in it, principally the poor, the weak and the redundant. Similar problems are, of course, still with us and will form the subject matter of later chapters. The great divide comes between those who believe that changes in the framework will be enough and those who believe the whole market system should be replaced.

The most sweeping doctrinal success of the classical period was *free trade*, the intellectual case for it having been fully established by 1815. The alleged earlier mercantilist view that the gain from trade consisted in a favourable trade balance was rejected as obtuse. As we have already noticed, Smith had shown the gain from free trade to consist in a more efficient allocation of resources and consequently a higher real income. Torrens and Ricardo devised the famous principle of 'comparative advantage' as an explanation of the pattern of trade and linked their argument with the 'law' of diminishing returns in agriculture to show that protection of agriculture would ultimately benefit landlords only, any benefit to profits or wages being swallowed up by the increasing rents that would be paid under competition. It so happened that the free trade case coincided with manufacturers' interests (in Manchester, if not in Birmingham) and popular versions of classical doctrine, so-called vulgarisation, by Bastiat in France and Cobden and Bright in England gained a strong hold. The well-known budgets of Huskisson, Peel and Gladstone seemed to show an inevitable progression towards free trade.

Nowadays one would expect an anti-free trade case to be argued, either on grounds of maintaining the level of employment or as a way of moving the terms of trade in a country's favour. The first argument was entirely absent from the mainstream of classical writing though it had certainly been in the minds of some mercantilist writers, just as it was to be in the minds of some Keynesians. Torrens, using a terms of trade argument, suggested that we should offer reciprocal, not unilaterial, free trade. But when the move to protection finally came at the end of the century it was as much due to financial and political causes as to economic ones.

Why was it that no restrictions on free trade (as in the labour market) were felt to be necessary on social grounds? Only the Tories, whose disinterestedness was suspect, expressed concern about those workers displaced from import competition industries.

MARKETS

The reason was an analytical one. Labour and other markets were assumed to adjust almost perfectly to chance disturbances, full employment of labour always being maintained. Apart from minor frictions workers displaced following a tariff reduction would be absorbed elsewhere almost at once. Thus apart from such things as defence, the only valid criterion for a trading policy was its efficiency.

Economic growth or capital accumulation required high rates of saving and therefore individual thrift in the context of stable money, good contract law and security of property. On this analysis the best contribution the state could make was to keep its activities to a minimum. Given this approach it is interesting to see what the mainstream classical writers had to say about Ireland; could the analysis of a rapidly growing capitalist economy be applied *in toto* to an under-developed country? Broadly speaking their answer was 'yes'. The classical view made itself felt not so much in the giving of reactionary advice on specific questions as in creating a general climate of opinion in favour of laissez-faire. It was a tragedy that Mill who, first with Thornton and then with Cairnes was prepared to admit the relative nature of economic theory, should find himself opposed in the House of Commons by those under the influence of the old dogmas.

Even so, the list of recommended changes in the framework was impressive—Catholic emancipation, reform of tithes, reduction of the established Irish Church, reform of the magistracy and extension of education. More interventionist solutions were on the whole rejected, the most impressive of these being in the Royal Commission of 1835. Senior was among the powerful but minority group of writers arguing the radical case. But public works were strongly resisted in principle by the most influential politicians, Peel, Russell and Gladstone. In practice, however, English politicians acquiesced in a central public works agency for Ireland as a lesser evil than more poor relief. Apart from public works and poor relief another solution was planned emigration but on this much more was said than done, the number of emigrants going through official channels being quite trivial. In any case, on a Malthusian view, emigration could only be seen as a temporary remedy, for any rise in real wages would soon cause a further increase in population.

RETROSPECT

It gradually became clear that a major change in the framework (land reform) was a necessary condition of success and after the disasters of 1846 quite radical solutions were canvassed. These had, in the course of the century, to contend with Irish landlords, the utilitarian view of freedom of contract and the obscurantism of much economic doctrine. And the old idea was slow in dying that economic progress could take place under laissez-faire once land consolidation had been achieved, on the English pattern. In view of this it is not surprising that the 1870 Irish Land Act disappointed the reformers. With hindsight it is possible to see that a judiciously selected mixture of all the principal remedies might have worked— the usual institutional reforms, land reform, public works to provide infra-structural investment, assisted emigration for those who wished it and adequate poor relief. But, taken together, such a mixture would have been an admission that 'market-plus-framework' was not a general precept for human affairs but merely of limited local application.

This brief discussion of a few interesting policy issues leaves the following impressions:

(1) The mainstream of political economy presumed in favour of laissez-faire within a stable institutional framework.
(2) Its effects on policy were important though operating in diverse and subtle ways.
(3) Minor currents of opinion taken together would have constituted an important opposition, but in practice they were never brought together in a coherent statement.
(4) Classical writers failed to produce a really convincing proof that competition must lead to socially desirable results.

The socialist opposition

The socialist alternative started by observing the poverty, hardship and degradation that accompanied 'capitalist' progress and then fanned out in several important directions—utopianism, reform and class polarisation. Utopianism is associated with Owen, Fourier and Saint-Simon. Owen, having despaired of the ignorance and apologetics of political economists, attempted to set up a community

47

in Indiana but with much less success than his paternalism at New Lanark. Fourier saw the industrial environment as the big enemy and suggested garden cities of four hundred acres, with workers owning the capital. Saint-Simon wanted a 'national workshop' organised by savants but retaining profits. The construction of 'utopias', ridiculed by more practical socialists, is again of great interest now that schemes for 'market socialism' are under active discussion in eastern Europe. But its great defect is its failure to say anything about how, *in a capitalist society*, such utopias could ever come about.

More practical and relatively moderate were the various attempts to achieve worthwhile reforms within the capitalist system: parliamentary reform, trade unions and cooperatives (the last two again being associated with Owen). At a theoretical level Thomas Hodgskin did a great deal to help the British working class movement by showing that the wages-fund concept was mistaken. The amount of consumer goods available for workers depends not on materials 'advanced' by capitalists but is provided out of what the workers currently produce. It is perfectly open to unions therefore to try to increase the share of consumer goods going to workers. In addition Hodgskin properly emphasised the conventional nature of property rights. As it happened, the marginalist theory of wages which had by the end of the nineteenth century replaced the old wage-fund doctrine was in some hands to be no less apologetic in character. The history of the British working class movement in the nineteenth century is well known. From my present standpoint the really important thing is that the mass of the movement was to be content with changes in the framework, particularly voting rights and trade union law, while accepting the free market system itself.

The third line of argument, polarisation, was most dramatically expressed in Marx's analysis of capitalism, though it had been suggested as early as 1824 by Thompson. (Polarisation is the process by which, under capitalism, society divides into two classes, a small number of rich capitalists and a large number of unemployed or badly paid workers.) Thompson also offered a recipe for the good society, believing that efficiency and justice could be simultaneously achieved by an alteration in the ownership of capital, 'it is great capitals that are wanted, not great capitalists'. Marx, basing his analysis on Ricardo, was able to reach his pessimistic conclusions about capitalism by combining a labour theory of value (goods exchange according to the socially necessary[1] labour used to make them) with a rapid and increasing rate of labour-saving technical advance. Free market economics, far from leading to social harmony, as claimed by the French economic journalist, Bastiat, would lead to revolution. As is often said, Marx left little in the way of a blueprint for the way in which a socialist society would operate, once established; there is more to be learned from some of Marx's socialist opponents, including Dühring, than from Marx himself.

The socialist opposition to classical laissez-faire was scattered with fundamental differences between the various writers. Certainly no comprehensive treatise was produced to rival the standard works of classical political economy.

British empiricism and the free market

This tradition is normally couched in a number of exceptions to the general principle of laissez-faire and I shall use it to link the names of J. S. Mill, Henry Sidgwick, Alfred Marshall and A. C. Pigou. Mill[2] started with a presumption that private enterprise was better than government activity for two reasons—it was more efficient and it was more conducive to liberty. It is hardly too much to say that his usual preoccupation with liberty was the bed-rock of his opposition. But it is characteristic of Mill that the list of exceptions to his basic proposition was formidable; roads, docks, harbours, canals, irrigation, hospitals, schools, colleges and printing presses could all be provided by the state under certain conditions. It should provide essential goods that individuals have no interest in providing, like lighthouses and buoys (and a 'learned class'!). It should protect

1   It is difficult to give a precise definition of this without becoming involved in the underlying pricing processes. It is, however, useful to think of socially necessary labour as labour used in an average efficient way.
2   For an account of Mill's changing attitude to socialism, see L. Robbins, *The Theory of Economic Policy in English Classical Political Economy*, London, 1952.

the interests of children. It should control monopolies, possibly (as in the case of water undertakings) by municipal ownership. It should provide favourable labour legislation. From a modern point of view his worries about joint-stock companies are most interesting, for Mill spotted the famous problem of a divorce between management and control. Not being directly responsible to shareholders, managers might become inefficient and their organisations bureaucratic. If this is so, there is not much to choose between private and state operation. Mill's analysis was untidy and seemed to have no clear guiding principle but was fully in accord with the eclectic fashion in which local government in particular was adopting a more active economic rôle in the mid nineteenth century.

Henry Sidgwick, the Cambridge academic, thought by some writers (including Schumpeter) to have been only a mediocre figure, is of importance at this stage. Adam Smith had argued that the 'invisible hand' would lead self-interested individuals to believe in the common interest. Though this was fascinating, Sidgwick argued, it had to be rejected. Self-interest does not maximise 'wealth', either in respect of the present (inventions, technical education) or of the future (the level of community investment). This was a notable shift in approach. Unlike Mill, Sidgwick was not starting with a presumption in favour of laissez-faire; he was stating, blankly, that competition was *not* efficient. He offered the double criterion of economic policy later to be taken up by Pigou:

(1) Maximum output per head,
(2) Just distribution.

Alfred Marshall, though a major figure in Anglo-Saxon economics, is mentioned here mainly for a negative reason. Typically he was very cautious about the rôle of the state in economic affairs. This showed up very clearly in his discussion of those industries which were subject to increasing returns (or decreasing costs). There might be a case, he admitted, for government encouragement of such industries but first of all a lot of careful research into supply and demand conditions would need to be undertaken. The value of Marshall in this period is the not unimportant one of refusing to lend his authority to simple laissez-faire remedies (in contrast to J. M. Clark in America).

Marshall's pupil, Pigou, started with Sidgwick's double criterion of economic policy arguing that any economic change should be implemented if it improves (1) without worsening (2), or improves (2) without worsening (1). Apart from erecting a sophisticated analysis of economic welfare on this simple base, Pigou stressed a phenomenon which has turned out to be of immense importance and to constitute a major criticism of laissez-faire (indeed it is the subject of a separate chapter in this book) the divergence between private and social costs. Practical illustrations can readily be multiplied, the standard Pigovian example being dirty factory smoke. A similar clash between private and social interest was due to monopolies which therefore needed some regulation. The cases that puzzled Pigou and that have continued to puzzle welfare economists ever since were those when his two criteria clashed. For instance, what should one do if a 'good' redistribution of income (by, say, raising the progression of the tax structure) would lead to a fall in output? Here is a clash between 'efficiency' and 'justice' and there is no objective way of bringing these under a common measure.

General equilibrium

It was in the context of a general equilibrium theory that a 'proof' of the efficiency of competition was eventually provided. This impressive analytical structure, whereby the behaviour of the economic system is represented in a model by a number of inter-dependent equations, was developed first by Walras[1] and then by Pareto, both at Lausanne. Walras satisfied himself that competition would lead to a 'best' solution insofar as it would enable individuals to maximise their utilities and firms to minimise their costs. But he shrank from laissez-faire on the grounds that one should introduce a social sector and make provision for monopolies and unjust income distributions. Pareto, very much more rigorously (and more elegantly) showed that competition would provide an efficient solution to the

---

1   L. Walras, *Elements of Pure Economics*, London, 1954.

economic problem (see Chapter 4). Pareto's own position on laissez-faire is not entirely clear. What is clear is that his work is the foundation of the whole of modern welfare economics, as the technical term Pareto-optimality frequently reminds us. The basis of general equilibrium theory was the marginalist 'revolution' of the 1870s, whereby the prices of goods were explained in terms of their marginal utilities and the prices of factors in terms of their marginal productivities. As marginal productivity was the contribution to output of one extra worker, J. M. Clark argued, a wage equal to the value of marginal product was fair. But competition produced this very result. Therefore competition was fair. Thus, according to this 'apologetic' view, competition performed the extraordinary feat of producing a result both efficient and fair. Opponents of laissez-faire found that they had even less to hope for from this brand of marginalism than they had from the old wages fund theory.

Unemployment

Up to the 'Keynesian' revolution of the 1930s, the orthodox teaching had been that apart from temporary trends (due to seasonal variations in demand, frictions and rapidly changing technology) there could be no substantial involuntary unemployment. An important group of writers (prominent among whom were Lauderdale, Malthus and, later, Hobson) had always insisted, for diverse reasons, that unemployment could arise from a deficiency of total demand. But mainstream classical writers held to various versions of Say's Law; that production generated incomes which generated demand so that a general deficiency of demand was impossible, even though individual producers might turn out to be mistaken in their expectations.[1] The same general presumption was maintained in neo-classical teaching. We require an explanation of this in terms of the 'free market'. Two markets,[2] the labour market and the money market, are of direct interest, the first determining the wage

---

1   Thus Ricardo in his *Notes on Malthus* expressed astonishment at Malthus' doubts about Say's Law.
2   See Chapters 3 and 4.

rate and the second determining the rate of interest. If there is high unemployment, as there was in British export industries in the 1920s, this could apparently be eliminated so long as workers were willing to accept lower wages, i.e. wage-cuts (public sector wages were in fact cut, following the May Committee, 1931). Neo-classical theory suggested that at lower wage rates producers would be willing to take on more labour. But, Keynes argued, it might prove impossible to reduce the real purchasing power of wages if prices followed money wages downwards. In this case it might be necessary to enforce a whole series of wage-cuts in an attempt to restore equilibrium in the labour market, and even this might not work.

Meanwhile total money demand would fall, entrepreneurs would find investment expenditure less profitable than before and curtail their own expenditure plans, the demand schedules in the various labour markets would shift to the left and the volume of output and employment would fall. The analytical defect of wage-cut arguments was the confusion between microeconomic and macroeconomic effects. It was disastrous to press the analogy between individual labour markets and the market for labour as a whole.

Opponents of the classical Say's Law had argued that savings were a leakage from the circular flow of expenditure. An increase in saving would therefore decrease total demand. Proponents of the law had countered that savings were indeed spent because they were converted into investment expenditure through loans markets. In neo-classical analysis the interest rate was the crucial 'price' which could adjust so as to bring the two into equality. If savings increased the supply schedule of loanable funds would move to the right, the interest rate would fall and producers would demand more funds for investment purposes while savings would be discouraged. At the new equlibrium more funds would be invested at a lower rate of interest.

The Keynesian attack on the relevance of this mechanism was twofold. Firstly the rate of interest was a *sticky* price. Keynes argued that the rate of interest is largely determined in the money market (principally the market for government bonds) and that it could not fall below a certain 'floor'. This floor depended on people's expectations about the future behaviour of interest rates. If there was a floor then it might prove quite impossible for the rate to go low enough to perform its neo-classical task. Secondly there was again a confusion between micro and macroeconomics. The savings schedule would alter as total income moved about. Thus there was no single equilibrium in the loans market but a series of equilibrium positions depending on the level of income.

The importance of Keynes's analysis was that the market mechanism (by way of movements in wage and interest rates) could not be relied upon to correct any given degree of unemployment. Indeed the economy could well remain at rest or in equilibrium with high levels of unemployment (an argument due first, I believe, to Mrs. Robinson). This crucial theorem is still intact despite various attempts to shake it. Policy implications were clear and important; it was quite legitimate for the state to interfere, by means of public works or whatever, in order to maintain full employment. The wage-cut argument (Pigou) and the condemnation of public works (Hawtrey, the Treasury, etc.) had both been refuted.

It is ironic that Keynes was regarded as a dangerous radical by the American right and as the saviour of capitalism by the European left. The relevance to the present book of Keynes's revolution is that one may go seriously astray by confining oneself to a microeconomic analysis. Free markets are not too good at solving the macroeconomic full employment problem. But my concern is almost entirely with microeconomic problems and I shall make the assumption, unless otherwise stated, that the central authorities can always intervene so as to maintain whatever level of macroeconomic activity they wish.

PART II

PIECEMEAL RULES

6 INTRODUCTION

A piecemeal policy is a rule or set of rules for decision-making in one part of an economic system, adopted with a view to improving economic welfare. Piecemeal policies are usually implicitly grounded in the basic theorem of welfare economics. Those we shall discuss are of major importance.

Externalities (Chapter 7)

The position analogous with competitive equilibrium is that marginal social costs and benefits should be equal to one another. The main types of externality are discussed along with various methods of taking them into account. One method is to impose a set of taxes and subsidies such that the market itself moves to the desired position, but for a wide range of problems this 'pseudo-market' solution will not do.

Pricing and investment criteria for public enterprises (Chapter 8)

The basic rule is simply lifted straight out of the list of conditions for competitive equilibrium, that is, that price should equal marginal cost of production. The meaning of this rule and its extension to problems of investment (or extending capacity) are considered. But I try to discuss in a very explicit way the assumptions underlying the marginal doctrine and what happens when they are relaxed. The discussion of assumptions in this chapter is basic to the whole section.

Cost-benefit analysis (Chapter 9)

This is not necessarily linked to a market economy, though in the British and American context costs and benefits are almost always valued in relation to market prices. The general principles of the analysis are presented in this chapter together with a survey and some areas of application. The analysis can be used in countries where the market system is poorly developed so long as somebody is prepared to put values on the costs and benefits. Additionally the factor services used may be valued at 'shadow prices' (see Chapter 11) rather than their actual prices. Thus cost-benefit analysis is probably a more versatile and more general tool than the text suggests. One must admit, however, that its growing acceptance in market economies is partly due to the apparently objective nature of money figures.

Second-best (Chapter 10)

A short discussion of the problem is offered with a survey of various solutions. The existence of the second-best problem is highly subversive to the present discussion; it implies a critique of piece-meal solutions. But it is absurd to push this critique too far. Is it really the case that a monopoly in the sale of candy-floss vitiates a marginal cost pricing policy for electricity or a present value investment policy for steel?

Taking the piecemeal policies together, one feels that the analogy with competitive equilibrium has had a beneficial effect. After all, a crude analogy with the business world would suggest profit maximising wherever possible. Competitive equilibrium turns out to have more to tell us about efficiency in the public sector than does the real world market process.

7 EXTERNALITIES (SPILLOVERS)

Externalities, long discussed by welfare economists, are now highly topical. They account for the difference between social cost and private cost and between social benefit and private benefit. For various reasons (principally that the gap between social and private cost has become more obvious) public opinion has been more sensitive to externalities in recent years.

Some side effects of economic activity may be a 'nuisance' for particular individuals. An unsightly rubbish tip, the smell from a chemical works, smoke and dirt from factory chimneys or noise from cars and aircraft may cause annoyance and displeasure; additionally, any one of them may constitute a health hazard. The creator of such external costs can usually avoid bearing most or all of them but they are nevertheless real. The main purpose of this chapter is to examine a few institutional devices whereby they may be taken into account. The chief justification for interference is that an *improvement* (in the sense of Chapter 4) can be made on the existing situation by encouraging markets to settle at the point where marginal social costs and benefits are equal instead of where (as under competition) marginal private costs and benefits are equal. It is worth emphasising that the externalities question is entirely separate, in principle, from any question of monopoly or second-best (see Chapter 10); it can arise even in a perfectly competitive situation and, so as to isolate its effects, I shall assume that competition prevails.

The reader will remember that two of the basic determinants of the whole set of prices and outputs were *preferences* and *production functions*. Under a decentralised régime it will be necessary that preferences and production functions can be split up in such a way that:

(1) Each consumer's satisfaction (or utility) depends *only* on the set of goods he can command,
(2) Each producer's output depends only on the set of inputs used.

Externalities occur wherever preferences or production functions cannot be split up in this way.

This type of definition readily suggests that a whole lot of apparent externalities can be dismissed as *pecuniary*. That an increase in car output requires more steel to be used is not a real externality as the extra steel has to be paid for and its cost taken into account by the car producer. A rough practical test is whether or not the cost (or benefit) will be taken into account by the ordinary working of the market.

Strictly speaking, only externalities that arise at the margin are relevant to economic efficiency (Pareto-optimality). Intra-marginal externalities are important from the income distribution standpoint but do not affect the marginal conditions. It is useful to call the former *relevant* externalities.

I now consider three main types of externality.

1. CONSUMPTION-TO-CONSUMPTION

My pleasure depends not only on the goods and services that I possess but also upon the goods and services that I know others to possess. I may be envious of one neighbour's new car but sympathetic to the poverty of another; jealousy and altruism are examples of externality. I can do nothing about this through normal market processes. If I feel strongly about the plight of the poor I can give money to charities, thus making both the poor and myself feel better-off and achieving an 'improvement'. Or I can vote for measures of poverty relief; indeed the type of welfare state possible, within the rules of social democracy, depends essentially on the altruism of the better off. If all the rich were altruistic, and not too attached to private charity, a proposal to increase taxation might command unanimous consent! The most obvious examples of consumption-to-consumption externalities occur within the family.

2. PRODUCTION-TO-PRODUCTION

Two parts of a single factory (or two factories) may be linked in such a way that the output of one depends partly upon the output of the other. For example, two road transport depots located close to one another may find that peak movements in and out of one depot create congestion costs for the other. Again the efficiency of one part of a steelworks may depend partly on the temperature at which the adjoining part is operated. Very many interdependences of this type are found *within* organisations; in fact they may be the main reason for having an organisation at all. To anticipate slightly the rest of the discussion the interdependent activities can be said to have been 'merged'. Thus the economist's favourite example is 'external economies of scale' (where the output of a single firm depends not only on its own inputs but on the output of the whole industry); but there is reason to believe that most important externalities of this type are swallowed up by mergers, i.e., internalised. Hence the paucity of real world illustrations.

3. PRODUCTION-TO-CONSUMPTION

This is by far the most interesting and important type of externality.[1] Nuisances and dangers (and pleasant experiences!) are generated as by-products of ordinary production in such a way that the market can take no account of them. The examples given on p. 59 are all of this class. Nuisances can almost always be avoided *at a cost*; pneumatic drills may be silenced, sewage may be properly treated, oil spillage may be prevented. Even where there is no apparent way of avoiding them this may be because no one has had the inducement to search for nuisance-avoiding innovations. Against the costs must be set the benefits. How is the balance to be struck?

A diagrammatic treatment

Suppose that a form of economic activity being pursued by (A) imposes external costs on some other party (B). Suppose further than the monetary value of the end product of this activity is P per unit and that P reflects its value to society. Let the marginal private cost of pursuing the activity be shown by the line MC_A and marginal social cost by MC_{A+B}. The difference between these lines (not shown in the diagram) is MC_B or the money value of the

---

1 For the sake of completeness one should mention a fourth category, consumption-to-production. The *consumption* benefits of, say, education might cause people indirectly to produce more.

externality at the margin. The level of activity is indicated by Q. In the absence of interference, Q will settle at Q_A where $P = MC_A$ and where profit is maximised. But it has already been implied that it would be an 'improvement' to move to the point where $P = MC_{A+B}$.

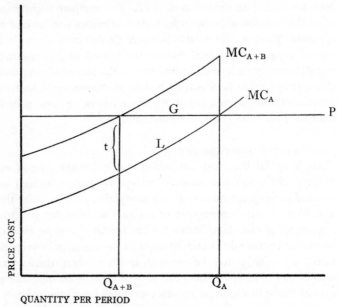

Fig. 3. Marginal Social Cost

Q would then settle at Q_{A+B}. What would be the extent of the improvement?

A loses (in money terms) the triangular area L. Over the range of output Q_{A+B} to Q_A he is foregoing profit on units he was formerly able to produce. B gains the whole area $G + L$. Remember that the external cost at the margin is the *difference* between the marginal cost curves MC_{A+B} and MC_A. This difference (over the appropriate range) is given by $G + L$.

The net money gain to society is therefore $G + L - L$ or simply G. This is as one would expect. Imagine that MC_A were removed from the diagram. Then a move from Q_A to Q_{A+B} would immediately lead to a gain of G. The obvious policy recommendation is to move to Q_{A+B} and much of what follows is devoted to various ways of getting there.

As usual, however, there are several important qualifications. Apart from the normal ethical postulate about distribution, there is the important question of how the overall gains G are distributed as between A and B. If the new position was reached by government fiat the gains and losses would indeed be as just set out. But this need not be so; generally, different methods of reaching Q_{A+B} will have different distributional effects. It is not logically possible, therefore, to advise the policy-makers to move to Q_{A+B} without at the same time accepting the distributional results of such a movement. Apart from this ethical question there are some technical difficulties.

(1) There is the usual difficulty about second-best. It might not be efficient to put price equal to marginal social cost in the Q sector when there are distortions in other parts of the system (see Chapter 10).

(2) There is the possibility that redistribution of income during the move to equilibrium will cause supply and demand conditions to alter in such a way that the equilibrum is itself changed. I shall assume that this effect is only of minor importance.

(3) There will be costs of implementing the change. If my garden is in a prominent position the flowers I grow may give pleasure to others and it would be an 'improvement' for me to increase the gorgeousness of my display. But if the cost of arranging for the change exceeds its net benefit it would no longer be an improvement to undertake it.

Solutions

Some of the main ways of ensuring that external effects are taken into account are:

(1) Merger   (4) Bargaining
(2) Regulation and fines   (5) Litigation,
(3) Taxes and subsidies

each of which is now described.

PIECEMEAL RULES

1. MERGER[1]

If we refer again to Figure 3, A and B may decide to pool their interests (perhaps by marrying or by forming a joint company). There are plenty of examples in the public sector. If two seaside resorts foul one another's beaches by discharging untreated sewage into the sea, a merger of the two local authorities would cause the external effects to be internalised. Similar considerations have influenced the amalgamation of river authorities and of police forces. A difficulty with the merger solution is that interests may overlap only in one or two aspects and the pattern of overlap may differ between one problem and another. Another difficulty is that mergers to deal with production-to-consumption externalities are very implausible. Further the costs of searching for 'improvements' in the post-merger situation may be very high.

2. REGULATION AND FINES

The government may decree that output shall not exceed Q_{A+B} in any period (or more probably that output of the nuisance by-product should not exceed a certain quantity). Economists usually express a dislike for this method on the grounds that it is crude and insensitive and would probably fail to locate Q_{A+B} at all precisely, given all the difficulties of getting the relevant information. It deprives the individual of an opportunity to incur *and pay* external costs. But it is a very good method whenever enforcement is easy and the benefits of restriction are large and obvious. Examples of such restrictions are the banning of the discharge of dangerous chemicals into rivers, the creation of smokeless zones and height restrictions on town centre buildings. Restriction is and will continue to be a most powerful weapon, especially in face of those large and terrifying externalities described by ecologists. Regulation must, of course, carry with it some sort of sanction. Thus, returning to the figure, it will pay A to disobey the regulation so long as the fine to be paid is less than L. One of the weak points of present legislation is that fines are rather low (for instance, a large fertiliser manufacturer was recently fined £50 for discharging chemicals into a

---

1 There are usually motives other than the internalising of externalities behind industrial mergers of the sort discussed in Chapter 14.

river). Regulation-plus-fines is, of course, a well-used method of traffic control.

3. TAXES AND SUBSIDIES

If a unit tax on output equal to 't' were imposed it would be in A's own best interests to produce an output equal to Q_{A+B}. Thus a judicious tax-subsidy device would permit actual production decisions to be taken on a decentralised basis. The tax is, of course, equal to the value of the externality at the margin; it converts marginal private cost into marginal social cost. The great difficulty is its calculation. One variant of the tax-subsidy solution, long advocated by economists, is road pricing (see Chapter 9) for which marginal social cost can be calculated relatively easily. This is much more flexible potentially than crude regulation, for the extent of the externality will vary from hour to hour and place to place. A suitable tax would decentralise the decision of whether or not to use cars for a given journey and lead motorists to adopt an 'improvement' (though remember the ethical caveats already mentioned). In a rather less sophisticated way, one subsidises those parts of the railway system that make losses from the 'private' standpoint (that is, the standpoint of British Rail) but nevertheless confer certain social benefits.

Whether the tax-subsidy method is suitable for particular cases depends almost entirely on the costs of gathering information and calculating the appropriate rate of tax.

4. BARGAINING

The two parties A and B might find it possible to bargain with one another. A must receive at least L in compensation if he is to agree to move; similarly B will be prepared to offer no more than G + L to induce A to move. The amount of compensation actually paid will lie between these limits. As a practical way of internalising externalities this method is most plausible when new rights are being negotiated. For instance, if a local authority's plan to build a new college on its periphery will have implications for the neighbouring authority's expenditure on roadworks, the relative burden on the two authorities may be settled by negotiation. Similarly two large firms, inflicting externalities upon one another, might be able to come to a mutually acceptable arrangement short of a merger. But the bargaining solution is not a great deal of use in the production to consumption case where those who bear the costs are disorganised and large in number. Notice that 'out-of-court' settlements are merely a special instance of the bargaining solution.

5. LITIGATION

B might sue A, through the courts, for the damages inflicted upon him (for instance, a government might sue an oil company for polluting beaches). If B's actions were successful and the damages accurately assessed, the end result would be that A would find it worthwhile to produce Q_{A+B}. Notice that B will not usually be willing to sue if costs are likely to be awarded to A and if these are large relative to the damages. This is a crude way of ensuring that only efficient adjustments are made but it has implications about the distribution of income.

It is possible, of course, to insure against damages. An oil shipping company might, for instance, insure against damages arising from spillage. But as an activity becomes more hazardous the premium to be paid will rise (this has happened in the case of very large oil tankers) and so discourage it. Indeed if damages are very high the activity might have to cease altogether! Litigation and the insurance principle together enable a price mechanism to work towards an efficient result.

Internalisation by litigation has at least two major drawbacks however. Firstly, in the production-to-consumption case, sufferers will often be scattered, badly informed and badly off. Legal aid is only a partial answer. One possibility (as happened in the case of oil pollution) is for the government to compensate sufferers in the first instance and then to seek redress from the oil companies. Secondly it will often be very difficult to attach monetary values to non-monetary costs. Present practice shows us that this is, though arbitrary, not impossible. The courts are in the habit of making assessments (admittedly crude and often inconsistent) of the cost of losing a limb, or one's sight, sexual powers or wife.

EXTERNALITIES

Edward Mishan[1] has called for a major extension of this approach in the form of recognised amenity rights. People would have a right to peace and quiet, to such things as a view, sunlight, 'clean' air and water, and would be entitled to sue anyone trespassing on this right. Road builders and aircraft operators would be forced to take 'externalities' into account and encouraged to look for alternative methods generating less nuisance. The underlying principle that externalities should be internalised is excellent, so is its automatic nature, for once legislation had been enacted decisions could be left to an entirely decentralised process. But it should be recognised that litigation is only one way of dealing with externalities. If it is to be widely used for amenity purposes some important preconditions must be met:

(1) That sufferers can readily identify the cause of the deterioration of their environment (this may be true for urban motorways but not where the nuisance is more diffuse, as in the case of urban atmospheric pollution).

(2) That generous legal aid is available.

(3) That legal processes are more widely available and more easily understood than at present (to this end it would be best to deal with amenity problems at a special type of court which had built up experience and a body of case-law). Unless income was first redistributed, the poor might do rather worse under this plan than otherwise.

These thoroughly desirable preconditions might make the litigation solution rather costly, but as a general line of attack on the problem they should be taken very seriously indeed.

Longer term externalities

The money values that people attach to various nuisances may, in the longer term, be less important than the whole question of

---

1   *Encounter*, Dec. 1959, pp. 3–13, gives a popular summary of Mishan's position.

conservation, pollution and the environment. Readers of *Silent Spring*[1] will not need reminding of the appalling results of in-discriminate use of pesticides and fertilisers. Some ecologists have found it useful to distinguish between the 'biosphere' and the 'technosphere'. The first is natural and is said to have an equilibrium of its own. The second is artificial (a word difficult to use non-pejoratively in this context!) and upsets the balance of the biosphere in an arbitrary and destabilising fashion. In particular the waste products of the technosphere are discharged in a form that the biosphere is unable to absorb.

Measuring costs, though desirable, is not the major problem. Basically the question involves a value judgement about the type of environment we wish to have; attempts to quantify may serve as a smokescreen behind which important decisions may be avoided. Adequate action will clearly have to be on an international scale and will, at various stages, involve the use of most of the main solutions already discussed. But the most versatile solution must be the adequate enforcement of fines coupled with strict regulations (our solution 2).

Policy

It is unwise to be dogmatic about which is the 'best' of the various solutions we have looked at; the search for a solution might proceed roughly as follows:

(1) Would the proposed change bring about an improvement, i.e., is $G > 0$? If so, consider all the solutions.
(2) Which solution is the cheapest to implement?
(3) Does G exceed the implementation costs of this solution? If so, consider the solution further. If not, decide on 'no action'.
(4) Does this solution have 'undesirable' effects on the distribution of income? If not, adopt the solution. If so, consider compensation.

---

1   Rachael Carson, *Silent Spring*, London, 1963.

EXTERNALITIES

The reader can doubtless try out this procedure in various ways. Consider smokeless zones. The answers would be:

(1) $G > 0$, probably.
(2) Solution (2), 'restriction-and-fines'.
(3) G exceeds implementation costs.
(4) Yes. But other solutions much less efficient. Compensate households and firms which have to change over fuels.

A final point can be made about policy. Externalities (as defined in this chapter) are inherent in the system, regardless of its form of organisation. Complete central control is the logical extreme of the merger solution; consequently, although it will in principle internalise all externalities, the implementation costs of doing so will be enormous. But rapid decentralisation of economic decision taking, without provision for devices to internalise externalities can lead to inefficiency. Externalities are essentially to do with decentralisation, not with capitalism.

8 PUBLIC ENTERPRISE

Investment by the nationalised industries in the U.K. is of the same order of magnitude as that by private industry. The nationalised sector now provides steel, electricity, gas, rail transport, postal and telecommunication services, coal, water and (soon) docks. Reasons for public ownership vary. Coal, transport and steel were, in the early post-war years, thought to be the 'commanding heights' of the economy. Gas and electricity could not conveniently be operated by private enterprise unless charters giving monopoly rights to certain companies (as with the early railways) were granted. Water resources have commonly been administered within the public sector on a local authority basis since the nineteenth century. How should one operate a public sector in an economy which still has a substantial private sector? I shall consider in this chapter the appropriate pricing and investment policies for nationalised industries.

The most relevant policy document is still the White Paper of 1967. Apart from exhortations to reduce costs, the paper concerned itself with the discounted cash flow technique of investment appraisal and with the policy of marginal cost pricing, both of which it recommended in a rather tentative way. It will be remembered that DCF is jargon for reducing costs and benefits to a 'present value' by the use of an appropriate discount rate. The paper recommended that this should be a standard way of testing an investment project for acceptance or rejection. An appropriate discount rate was thought to be 8% (roughtly equivalent to the return on a safe investment in private industry); this was raised to 10% in 1969 in view of the continuing upward drift in interest rates generally. Many projects would, of course, be acceptable by a large margin. These excesses would serve to meet various financial targets which were to be negotiated with the individual industries. Acceptance or rejection of projects was not to be rigid, however, and permission would be given for 'uneconomic' projects that were justified on social grounds. Indeed the accounts of British Rail were to be split up to make this distinction clear.

As for pricing, 'in addition to recovering accounting costs, prices need to be reasonably related to costs at the margin'. The recovery of costs was thought to be an essential part of financial discipline (even though it might conflict with the marginal cost principle). Enterprises might be allowed to depart from marginal costs in the case of peak demands (as in electricity) but the practice of 'cross-subsidisation' (allowing surpluses in some parts of an industry to cover deficits elsewhere) was to be discouraged, except on social grounds. Thus in a modest and undogmatic fashion the government accepted, as part of policy, a theoretical tool long advocated by some economic theorists.

Marginal cost pricing

Fundamental questions about the ethical basis of economics are raised by a marginal cost pricing policy. I would like to shelve these for the present by making a number of assumptions, and the discussion will be mainly about the operation of a single public enterprise producing a single commodity. The assumptions are:

(1) Conditions appropriate to perfect competition prevail throughout the whole of the rest of the economic system,
(2) Consumers are the best judges of their own interests,
(3) The distribution of incomes is equitable,
(4) There are no relevant externalities.

The meaning and importance of these assumptions should be clear to the reader from Chapter 4. I shall discuss the consequences of relaxing them later in this chapter.

It will be recalled that one of the conditions of efficient output is that price should equal marginal costs of production. This was supposed to be a general condition, so it should apply to public as well as private enterprise. The implication is that managers of public enterprises, like their counterparts in a market socialist system (see Chapter 13), should be instructed to follow the iterative procedure:

—equate price with marginal cost,
—equate output with demand at that price.

71

The instruction implies an iterative process. Managers will set a level of output and charge a price equal to marginal cost. At this price the market may or may not be cleared, and price and output have to be adjusted until it is. Whenever demand or cost conditions change, price and output will have to be altered.

This proposition is a corollary of the 'basic theorem' of welfare economics (see Chapter 4). An alternative justification (in terms of the 'public interest') will be given in a moment. A rough case can also be made out on commonsense grounds. Marginal costs represent the value of the resources used up in making an extra unit of output and are therefore appropriate guides to choice. A price equal to marginal cost will face the consumer with the real consequences, or *opportunity costs*, of his decisions. This can be particularly important at peak periods (of travel, electricity consumption, etc.), when marginal costs are much higher than average costs. Contrariwise, it can also be important when marginal costs are low. Thus the marginal cost of using a bridge is approximately zero, while the average cost may be substantial. It would seem 'unfair' or 'unreasonable' in these situations to put price equal to average cost.

Average cost pricing can, additionally, be shown to encourage absurd decisions. Suppose a factory is producing both nuts and bolts and that the whole undertaking is profitable. Suppose now that the firm's accountants advise it to allocate all its overhead or fixed costs between nuts and bolts on an arbitrary 50:50 basis. Suppose it turns out that the receipts for bolts fall short of their costs, thus calculated. The output of bolts is then discontinued, as they are an unprofitable line. But the *whole* of overheads have then to be borne by nuts and if these in turn are therefore unprofitable the whole enterprise has to pack up! This rather extreme example should be read as a warning; that average cost pricing encourages the arbitrary allocation of overhead costs among products and may lead to irrational output policies. The analysis of the celebrated Beeching Report came dangerously near to this in its treatment of the economics of branch lines.[1]

---

1   See, for example, *The Reshaping of British Railways*, British Railways Board, H.M.S.O., 1963.

A simple consequence of marginal cost pricing should be mentioned here. It would be wrong to raise price above cost marginal merely in order to obtain revenue for further investment; the managers would simply act as monopolists and set price above marginal cost depending on the price elasticity of demand. But this would violate the marginal cost pricing rule as just described. In addition it would have interesting redistributive implications. Consumers of the commodity instead of the tax payer would be financing investment expenditure. How seriously one takes this criticism depends partly on how seriously one takes the question of second best (see Chapter 10).

A 'surplus' criterion

Pursuit of maximum profit is not an appropriate policy for a public enterprise. Is it possible to set out an objective of the same broad kind as profit maximisation? Various criteria involving the concept of a 'surplus' have been put forward as indicating the public interest. Let us define the concept *net surplus*:

$$\text{net surplus} = \text{total surplus} - \text{total costs}.$$

Perhaps it can be best understood in terms of a diagram (Figure 4). Total surplus is the gross benefit derived by consumers from their consumption; a monetary measure of this benefit is provided by the whole area under the demand schedule, from the origin to the level of consumption or output. It is the sum of the maximum amounts the consumers would be willing to pay, or marginal demand prices, and is given, at the level of output D, by the whole area OBCD in the figure. Remember that marginal cost is defined as the *extra* cost of producing extra units of output. Thus total costs are represented by the area under the marginal cost curve OACD. Net surplus is therefore given by the shaded area,

$$\text{ABC} = \text{OBCD} - \text{OACD}.$$

The reader will be able to satisfy himself, by inspection, that net surplus is, in fact, largest at the level of output D. (At levels of output higher than D, cost increases faster than total surplus, and at

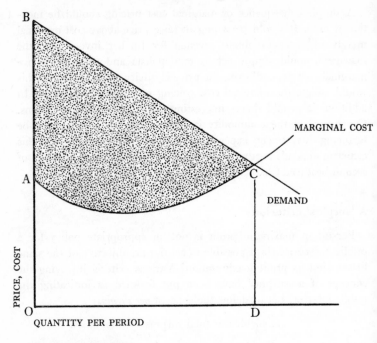

Fig. 4. Net Surplus

levels lower than D, cost falls less rapidly than total surplus.) The manager of the enterprise would also arrive at this output if he followed the double rule already given.

There are many snags about this surplus concept, both theoretical and empirical; the most substantial from the present point of view is that it requires knowledge of the *whole* of the demand schedule (otherwise the areas could not be measured) while a manager operating the double rule would need only know something about the demand schedule in the immediate neighbourhood of current output levels. This drawback is less serious when we move on to consider investment policies, for it then becomes important to have more information about the demand schedule in any case. Bearing in mind the assumptions (1) to (4) above, net surplus does not serve too badly as an objective function.

74

Which marginal costs?

Marginal costs are likely to be very different, depending on the period of time being considered. A few hundred extra commuters could be carried during the London rush hours by altering schedules, putting on extra trains (if available), by crowding and overtime working. The extra cost per commuter, to the railway system, is likely to be quite high. But if major investments have been made in such as new track, the extra cost of carrying those same few hundred commuters, on a regular basis, might be very much less. In the same way, the extra cost of electricity at peak hours during the winter period would be high, given the present network of generators. But a similar increase with a much expanded system would be far less expensive. Which marginal cost is relevant?

A suitable policy presentation (provided in the last decade or so by a number of distinguished French economists) is as follows. *The enterprise should charge a price equal to short run marginal costs up to the limits of capacity. At capacity it should simply charge a market clearing price. It should then follow an investment policy based on the present value criterion. In full equilibrium it will turn out that price equals long run marginal cost.* Full equilibrium is where managers do not wish to increase capacity further. The present value criterion has already been described in Chapter 3. Again the analysis can be most easily understood by means of a diagram (Figure 5). A marginal cost curve of an extremely simple type has been chosen for the sake of exposition. Let marginal operating and maintenance costs be given by the horizontal line SMC (short run marginal costs). These are releavnt only up to the level of full capacity, Q_1.

According to the rule described, price would be set equal to SMC for levels of output up to Q_1. But at Q_1 no more output can be produced (given capacity). If demand is as shown in the figure (and expected to remain so), a price equal to SMC would leave some demand unsatisfied; there would be queues or rationing (which in the case of electricity would take the form of load shedding or power cuts). A market clearing price would be P_1.

But this exceeds SMC by the amount α per year. As long as the new capacity costs less than α (capacity cost being expressed as an

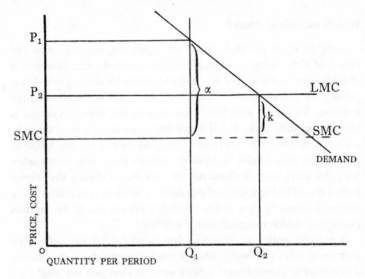

Fig. 5. Short and Long Run Marginal Cost Pricing

annuity[1]) it will be worth buying more capacity. The cost of capacity is assumed to be k, the difference between LMC and SMC so that $\alpha > k$ and investment takes place. Thus the result of setting price at market clearing level at full capacity and adopting a form of present value investment criterion is that managers extend capacity up to Q_2 at which P_2 is charged.

What would have happened had a policy of $P = LMC$ been adopted? If it had been combined with adjustment of output so as to equate supply and demand, Q_2 would also have been reached by this route.

---

1 At capacity levels up to Q_2 present value of annual benefits (best measured as 'surplus') minus present value of operating and maintenance costs would exceed the cost of new plant, at the going discount rate. Annual capital costs and therefore long run marginal costs can, if desired, be calculated by reducing capital costs to an annuity. If the cost of capital is K and the rate of discount i then K can be expressed in terms of an annuity k where

$$K = k/i$$

In the end, therefore, at full equilibrium, it makes no difference whether the manager operates the rule already described or simply sets price equal to long run marginal cost. In practice the market clearing price tends to be modified fairly gradually towards long run marginal cost; the process of reaching equilibrium seldom gets very far before a fresh set of disturbances is felt. Also, in practice, a continuous fine adjustment of capacity is rarely possible and it may be necessary to undershoot or overshoot the optimum when equipment is 'lumpy' or indivisible. Lastly, notice that the rule described is perfectly consistent with the pursuit of a net surplus criterion.

Capacity is sometimes shared between different types of consumer (for example, users of electricity at different times of the year). The problem of how to allocate such costs between them is a variation on the old problem, already referred to, of allocating fixed costs. Technically it is known as the 'shifting peak' problem and it presents many difficulties. It is not appropriate, therefore, in an introductory discussion of this kind to present a detailed analysis. Suffice it to say that one way (but not the only way) is to allocate the costs according to the relative strengths of demand by the various groups of consumers. Thus those travellers using trains at the very peak would bear a larger share of capacity costs than travellers during only moderately busy periods; and those passengers travelling off-peak would only be expected to pay running costs.

Losses and two-part tariffs

Whenever fixed costs are high in relation to variable costs there is a possibility that an enterprise using a marginal cost pricing rule would actually make losses. The purist view is that this does not matter; the aim is efficiency not just book-keeping. Profits and losses are merely transfers of income between groups. But the purist view has come under attack for several reasons:

(1) Orthodox opinion is allergic to the pursuit of vague goals like 'efficiency' or 'maximum net surplus', preferring a comfortable balance of the books. More importantly, financial discipline (probably in the form of target rates of return on capital) is

useful from a managerial point of view. Those at various stages in the chain of command know what is expected of them and are able to compare their performance with that of others inside and outside their organisation.

(2) If losses are financed out of taxation the imposition of income or purchase taxes will upset marginal equivalences elsewhere in the system and possibly lead to inefficiency in the allocation of labour and other resources.

(3) Losses imply a redistribution of income from taxpayers to a group of consumers. This may or may not be desirable on social grounds.

A convenient device that permits marginal cost pricing together with a profit in this type of case is the so-called 'two part tariff'. The consumer pays a fixed charge per period (say per quarter, as in the cases of electricity and telephone services) plus a charge that varies with the amount of use. Clearly it must not be possible for consumers to resell the product to one another thus escaping most of the fixed charge. The variable charge will normally reflect marginal cost only in a rough and ready sort of way but some sensitivity can be obtained at little extra expense. Thus the electricity boards allow off-peak electricity at lower prices (reflecting lower marginal costs of production) and telephone calls are cheaper in the evenings and at weekends. In many countries (principally the U.S.A.) water, too, is subject to marginal cost pricing under a two part tariff. In the U.K. domestic consumers pay an annual water-rate only, so that marginal cost to the user is zero (minor exceptions include a charge for hoses, etc.). But the marginal cost of production is very high and many economists argue for the metering of water. More generally the trouble is that pricing devices can be made more sensitive only at extra cost; one should not ignore the marginal costs of marginal cost pricing. Thus the price of telephone calls or electricity might (at large expense) be made to vary continuously during the day depending on the 'load'. The fixed charge is normally based on some simple rule of thumb, even though the supplier usually has monopoly power and could perhaps drive harder bargains with some individuals than others. A two-part tariff has been suggested for other services, buses for example. The holder of a special card (which he has paid for and which is available only to himself) would present it to an automatic device on the bus and pay an extra charge depending on travel conditions. At peak periods he would pay rather a lot, at off-peak periods very little. But for a wide range of goods it would be difficult to prevent customers buying at marginal rates and reselling to others. In these cases a price that is proportional to, but greater than, marginal costs may be appropriate.

Costs

The question of the relationship between price and marginal cost, though important, must not be allowed to obscure the need to produce any given output at lowest cost. Hairbreadth distinctions about the former are of no value if there is widespread inefficiency on the cost side. It might, of course, be necessary to retain inefficient techniques or to phase them out only slowly for social reasons (to ease the impact of redundancy, for instance). But generally the manager of a nationalised industry should, like the capitalist entrepreneur and the manager of a fully socialist enterprise, be constantly searching for new methods and ways of reducing cost. The justification for this is that materials and other resources are released for use in other parts of the economy. Such searching requires an incentive of some kind, possibly based on profit but not necessarily so. Thus the manager could gain by reducing cost if he were paid according to net surplus produced. This search procedure is an essential part of the case for free market capitalism, though strangely under-played by most of its advocates.

Wider implications

At this stage we should notice the consequences of relaxing the assumptions listed earlier in the chapter.

1. *Competitive conditions prevail elsewhere.* To relax this assumption is highly damaging. On the other hand it is a blatantly unrealistic one. If there *is* a departure from competition somewhere

in the rest of the system (a little monopoly here, a tariff or two there) the manager of the public enterprise cannot be sure that he is doing the right thing by putting price equal to marginal costs. The prices which he pays for his inputs and the price which he will get for his output all differ from what they would have been under competition. By putting his price equal to marginal cost he may even be making the overall situation worse! This proposition, which is examined in Chapter 10, is known in the theoretical literature as the theory of second best.

2 and 3. *Consumers are the best judges of their own interests and the distribution of incomes is equitable.* Between them these assumptions justify consumer sovereignty. Remember that even the non-profit criterion introduced, net surplus, relies heavily on knowledge of the demand schedule, both for pricing and for investment decisions. That the case for complete consumer sovereignty is weak is general to almost every problem discussed in this book, but it has special relevance to marginal cost pricing. One of the key points made in the White Paper quoted earlier in this chapter was the undesirability of 'cross-subsidisation'. This involves some goods being sold at less than marginal cost and others at more than marginal cost, a practice that was condemned unless undertaken for definite and explicit 'social' reasons. A lot of cross subsidisation, especially within British Rail and the postal and telecommunications services, had grown up more or less at random, certainly without a clear rationale. But it is very important indeed that the abolition of these unintended forms of subsidy should not harm those activities that require subsidy on social grounds—the maintenance of uneconomic pits by the Coal Board so that redundancy is only gradually achieved with minimal social harm, letter deliveries in remote country areas, for instance. Apparent cross-subsidies may also be justified on externality grounds; more of this in a moment.

The argument that consumers are not good judges of their own interests (while powerful in the cases of education, health, housing and other welfare or semi-welfare activities) is not of major significance in commodities like fuel, transport, postal services, etc. More important is the uneven distribution of income. Old people may die of cold in the same winter that there is no great 'demand' for coal, or they may not be able to get into a shopping centre because the buses do not 'pay'. The classic answer, that rather than subsidise particular services one should increase incomes, is not particularly comforting in the short term when incomes have patently failed to increase. Until a more equitable distribution of income is achieved it is perfectly proper to offer fuel or public transport freely or cheaply.

4. *There are no relevant externalities*. The most obvious ones in the public sector are associated with transport (discussed in greater detail in Chapter 9). Consider the closing of an uneconomic branch line of British Rail. To the rail authorities the benefit from closing the line is cost avoided and the 'cost' is revenue foregone. But there will be other costs (principally traffic congestion on the roads) not borne by the authorities. Similarly the construction of the Victoria Line in London was expected to yield high benefits in terms of reduced congestion on the *roads*. The landscaping of old mining areas (or careful demolition of old railway stations) is unlikely to occur if left to public enterprises *even if* a marginal cost pricing and a present value investment policy is pursued. For the benefits are social while the costs are 'private' (i.e., they concern the decision making agency). If public enterprises are instructed to take external effects into account, the net effect will probably be larger deficits which the government would have to be prepared to finance.[1]

Measurement

Even if we ignore externalities and the wider social issues the problem of measuring marginal cost is immense. In a general discussion it is easy to produce convincing general rules (such as 'price equals marginal cost') but, in practice, simple rules tend to crumble in the hands of even the most conscientious planner. There are many reasons for this. Firstly there is uncertainty. This affects both the demand side and the cost side. Even after sophisticated econometric analyses one cannot be sure that forecasts of demand,

---

1   *Railway Policy*, H.M.S.O., Cmnd. 3439, 1967.

and therefore investment programmes, will turn out to be correct. Under-estimation of the demand for electricity is a celebrated case. Uncertainty also affects the cost side. One cannot be certain about the rates of technical advance or the future prices of materials. Then there are political uncertainties. Secondly there is the question of sheer complexity. The single enterprise making a homogeneous product is a convenient myth. A nationalised undertaking will be an enormously complex industrial system producing a large number of different products. Even with the aid of operational research and systems analysis it is exceedingly difficult to get a simple measure of something like 'marginal cost'. Thirdly there is the cost of information gathering. In a complex system the cost of making more precise measurements of costs and benefits could be prohibitive. Rules-of-thumb that work fairly well and produce reasonably sensible results may be better than something more sophisticated.

Summary

The importance of the nationalised industries makes it desirable that they have rational pricing and investment policies. A well-known prescription is the marginal cost pricing principle which can be shown to be an efficient rule under certain fairly severe assumptions. It can also be established with the aid of a 'net surplus' instead of a 'profit' criterion. A modified form of short run marginal cost pricing together with a 'present value' investment criterion leads eventually to long run marginal cost pricing. The problem of losses can be met to some extent by forms of two-part tariffs. When certain simplifying assumptions are relaxed it is seen that marginal cost pricing cannot be considered in isolation from broader social issues. Finally the problems of empirical measurement must not be underestimated.

9 COST-BENEFIT ANALYSIS

Cost-benefit analysis is an aid to rational decision-taking in those areas where market mechanisms are for various reasons inappropriate. We suggested in the previous chapter some rules (marginal cost pricing and the present value investment criterion) for the conduct of nationalised industries in those cases where it is possible to charge the user. Are there similar rules for taking decisions about those activities from which the whole community benefits? Such activities are river management, road construction, urban renewal, preservation of the countryside and accident prevention. Sometimes it is not possible to draw the boundaries sharply (road-tolls) but I have in mind those goods that are collectively provided and from which people cannot (or should not) be excluded. Theoretically they could be organised on a small community basis through bargaining processes but, as the costs of agreement are likely to be high, our concern will be almost entirely with provision by the state and its various organs.

General problems of approach and technique are discussed in this section and the rest of the chapter sketches some of the approaches made so far to some specific types of problem.

Analysis

The basic procedure of cost-benefit analysis (CB) is as follows:

(1) Draw up a list of alternative projects,
(2) List all the costs and benefits associated with each project,
(3) Quantify the costs and benefits as far as possible,
(4) Calculate a money valuation of the costs and benefits,
(5) Submit the final valuations.

A few words must be said about each of these.

1. The apparently simple instruction to draw up a list of alternative projects is really of immense importance and is becoming standard CB procedure. To the CB analyst it is perfectly natural

that several alternatives should exist, but to his client this often seems heretical! Busy decision-makers usually settle for a particular project at a rather early stage in the planning process and feel themselves to be under personal attack when it is suggested that a few alternatives also be considered (this seems to be particularly true in the field of urban planning). At the time of writing, the Roskill Commission is having a second look at the whole question of the site of a third London Airport—with alternatives. The constant pressure to look at alternatives is a major contribution of CB. Of course, this is more costly than it would be to study just one project, though research costs of all kinds are usually trivial in relation to the total costs of such projects.

2. The list of costs and benefits must be comprehensive; all costs and benefits must be included no matter to whom they accrue. In principle this gets over one of the great difficulties about the market mechanism, that it is not very good at dealing with externalities (see Chapter 7). Thus one of the main benefits of the Victoria Line in London was that it allegedly cut journey times of *surface* traffic. Flood prevention schemes usually help *everyone* in a river basin. In practice there are limits as to how far one can go; the ripples from any development scheme soon become too small to be worth counting. Again, the standard procedure is valuable in itself. It causes the planner to reflect on the wider implications of what he is doing and to search for information which he would not otherwise have bothered with.

3. Listing of costs and benefits is very closely linked with their quantification. Quantification is *not* the same as valuation. It is technical rather than economic. By how many minutes will a new road reduce journey times? How much extra water will a new dam provide? How many people will hear the noise from supersonic aircraft? CB has given a very big push to this type of quantification. These two planning stages, 2 and 3, represent between them a useful clarification, even if the analysis is not taken further.

4. Valuation presents the greatest problems.
(a) There is the question of technique. We do not need to present

any new tools of analysis at this stage, as the two main pieces of technique have already been discussed.

Investment appraisal will be made with the aid of the present value analysis already described in Chapter 3. It will be convenient sometimes to use the internal rate of return instead. The reader is reminded that the criterion is

$$NPV > 0 \quad \text{or} \quad R > i.$$

The investment criterion by itself tells us nothing about how to value the benefits and costs themselves. A useful technique here is the 'net surplus' concept already described in Chapter 8. The reader will remember that the use of marginal cost pricing is consistent with the net surplus criterion. When pricing is inappropriate it will still be rational to push the provision of a service to the point at which the marginal costs and benefits are equal to one another. Net surplus, it will be remembered, is defined as

$$\text{net surplus} = \text{total surplus} - \text{total costs.}$$

(b) There is the question of how to value non-marketable benefits. The general principle followed is to use valuations as revealed by actual behaviour; this is on the whole preferable to simple opinion-seeking. Thus people's valuation of journey time is based as far as possible on their actual choice between alternative routes. The following is a crude illustration. A commuter can choose between two modes of transport, car and bus. The journey by bus is a quarter of an hour longer than that by car but 5 new pence cheaper. If he elects to go by car we may infer that he seems to value time at least at 20 new pence an hour. On this basis it is possible to construct a *surrogate* demand curve for various types of service, a curve which shows how consumers would behave if the service were indeed marketable.

(c) It will prove impossible to put a money valuation on some of the costs and benefits. These are usually referred to as '*intangibles*'. Though analysts are making great strides towards quantifying the unquantifiable, beauty, peace and human life remain largely inviolate. The only thing to be done about intangibles is to list them for the decision-maker's consideration.

(*d*) It will often be useful to do a *sensitivity* analysis. For many of the valuations there will be no unique answer. One should then consider a whole range of plausible assumptions and make estimates of how changes or errors would affect the final valuation. It may turn out to be rather sensitive to variations in some of the assumptions but not to others. This point can be illustrated by CB analyses of motorway construction. The result is not very sensitive to small changes in the assumption about the length of useful life of the new road; the present value of changes in very distant costs and benefits is small indeed (see Chapter 3). But the result *is* sensitive to small changes in the assumption about journey time valuation. Clearly it will not be worth estimating net benefit on alternative assumptions about factors that do not greatly affect the final outcome.

5. Results can be presented to the decision-maker as a set of present values or rates of return. On the face of it he has simply to choose the highest of these but in fact his job must be rather more subtle than this. For one thing, he might have to take political and other pressures into account and to strike a balance between questions of economic efficiency and questions of power and tradition. The importance of these very real considerations should not be under-emphasised. For another, he will have to make up his mind about the list of 'intangibles'. Lastly, he may be presented with a range of assumptions, as we have just suggested. He also has to make up his mind about which of these is 'best' or 'most realistic'. But the additional freedom granted to him is not a licence to make the decision on a purely arbitrary basis. For the bunch of assumptions he selects has to be applied right across the board; if he is going to cheat he will have to be fairly sophisticated about it (especially if the summary cost-benefit analysis is to be published!).

Readers with experience of real life decision-making processes will hardly recognise them in the rather idealised picture I have presented. The main simplification I have made is to assume that the expert is much more detached than he could ever really be. In his work he seems to make no value judgements; he is merely a maker of calculations and measurements, a demonstrator of the consequences of alternative schemes. In practice it is more subtle. The expert imbibes values from his masters during their early contact (and vice-versa). His very presentation of the results may be constructed so as to tip the decision one way or the other. Then again the really drastically different alternatives (like public versus private transport) may have been discarded at a highly crucial earlier phase in the planning process, possibly even before experts had been called in. For this reason some writers have suggested that a study of the generation of alternative schemes would be of even greater interest than studies of the alternatives themselves.

Flood damage

Flood prevention is often part of a larger scheme, including perhaps irrigation and the provision of hydro-electric power. Whenever this is so the scheme must, of course, be analysed as a whole. For the sake of simplicity we consider flood prevention alone. On the costs side, things are relatively simple. There will be capital costs plus maintenance costs of whatever construction work is needed. Only two complications need be considered here.

(1) In order to achieve any given level of prevention there will often be a choice of 'techniques'. For instance, one might provide a low dam up river plus major deepening of the river bed, or a high dam up river plus minor deepening of the river bed; or extra embankments might be weighed against both of these. The best method will, of course, depend on relative prices, including the discount rate.

(2) There may be a case for valuing resources, particularly labour, at other than market price. Thus national wage agreements will prevent the hiring of very cheap labour; but if there is unemployment in the area the 'shadow price' of labour will be lower than the wage rate (on shadow prices see Chapter 11). In this case the 'opportunity' cost of employing labour is low and apparent costs should be marked down accordingly. The practical effect of this rule, if implemented nationally, would be to encourage construction work in

areas of unemployment. Attempts to put an actual figure on the shadow wage, however, have been rare.

Benefits consist of costs avoided; prevention of crop and livestock losses, loss of property, loss of life, etc. Flood damage is not the same each year, there will be bad years and good years. In a typical year, therefore, the expected benefit will be the probability of damage avoided. If there is £1m of damage one year in 10, and £100,000 of damage for the other 9 years, the mathematical expectation of damage in any year will be £190,000.[1] For most river basins flood records go back quite a long way so there will have been enough observations to permit the calculation of rough probabilities. A relatively new technique is to devise computer simulations of a river's flood history. The use of probabilities is in accord with the common belief that if damage is likely to occur only rarely, then it is not 'worth' making a provision for it.

Crops and livestock damaged or destroyed can be measured in terms of loss of market value. The same is true of property. Attempts to put a money value upon human life have been made but the subject is controversial and probably best avoided in an introduction of this type. A point of general interest is that if one does count such things as loss of crops, one should not in addition include loss in land value. For the value of land is simply the present value of expected net rentals; to count the loss in net rentals (due to crop loss, etc.) and also the loss of land value would be to double-count.

Estuarial barrages

The steady rise in U.K. incomes and population, together with an uneven geographical distribution, has led water authorities to search for new sources of supply. One such source is the estuarial barrage, for which 'desk-studies' have already been undertaken at Solway and Morecombe. These studies are interesting because they envisage comprehensive schemes with benefits of several different types. The scheme discussed below, while based on the desk-studies, is imaginary.

---

1   $(1/10 \times £1,000,000) + (9/10 \times £100,000)$.

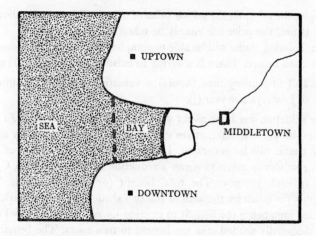

Fig. 6. Estuarial Barrage

The barrage will contain a large freshwater lake from which supplies can be pumped to a nearby conurbation. Along the top of the barrage will be a new road, thus making it possible for through traffic from the north and south to avoid Middletown. The muddy flats in the bay near Middletown can be reclaimed by building an additional small barrage. (The reader will easily be able to think of other possible benefits or disadvantages such as recreation, bird watching.) Costs and benefits can then be set out.

Costs	Benefits
1. Original construction costs 2. Maintenance	1. Extra water supply 2. Fall in journey times 3. Land reclaimed

The benefits can be valued as follows:

1. Extra water will be sold to the extracting authorities at the appropriate number of pence per thousand gallons, depending on the strength of demand. If the new supply is large in relation to existing

supply, the effect on the selling price of water will have to be allowed for. If not, the price can simply be taken as given.

2. Existing traffic will be able to complete the journey in a shorter time than before. There is a saving to existing users (per year) of

Fall in journey time (hours) × valuation per hour × number of journeys per year (j).

The valuation per hour might vary within a range of 25p to £1 per hour—in any case alternatives can be presented. Additionally some new traffic will be generated. In Figure 7 the construction of the new roadway is taken to mean a reduction in the cost (from C_1 to C_2) of each journey. The total benefit (or total change in 'net surplus') is given by the sum of the two shaded areas, the vertically shaded area being the benefit to existing users (as given above) and the diagonally shaded area the benefit to new users. The benefit to new users is approximately

$\frac{1}{2}$ × fall in journey time × valuation per hour × number of new journeys (j).

Thus savings in journey time (per year) to both new and existing users can be measured in money terms (approximately) by the sum of these two areas.

3. The value of land reclaimed will depend on its planned use. If demanded for agricultural purposes it might be worth, at current prices, up to £300 per acre; if demanded for housing it could command over £10,000 per acre and very much more than this if demanded for commercial purposes.

The job of the CB analyst would be to work out net present value on various assumptions and under various specifications of the scheme. It would then be possible to accept or reject the scheme or to compare it with other schemes.

Noise

Noise (especially from motor vehicles and aircraft but also noise experienced by industrial workers) is a 'nuisance externality'. It can usually be reduced *at a cost*. Thus if a noise is described as 'necessary' or 'unavoidable' the implication is that the cost of reducing it is

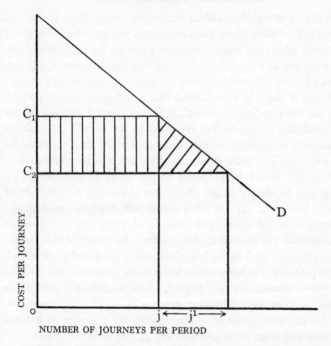

Fig. 7. Cost Savings to Generated and Existing Traffic

greater than the value of any benefits which might follow. Recent public interest in the noise problem has led to a new interest in the development of effective silencers for pneumatic drills, aero-engines and so on. The extent to which people regard noise as a nuisance is highly important for decisions about the size and location of, for instance, a new airport. Some cost-benefit analysts have tried to put a money valuation on this dislike.

Surprisingly, some people (up to 30%) seem remarkably tolerant of noise, but on the whole those who live very near main traffic thoroughfares or near major airports would much prefer to be without it.[1] The physical problem of actually measuring noise is

---

1 *Noise from Motor Vehicles* (The Wilson Report), H.M.S.O., Cmnd. 1780, 1962–3.

not quite as straightforward as one might hope. Even so, several methods of valuation have been suggested. Before considering these it is worth asking the basic question—what are the implications of a very high cost of noise? Welfare economics (see Chapter 4) suggests that if all those adversely affected by noise are adequately compensated and if there is nevertheless still a net gain from a project, there has been an 'improvement'. If there is no net gain (no matter how profitable or convenient it would be for certain groups, like transatlantic air passengers) then to go ahead with the project would be inefficient. The basic principle of valuation is to establish how much people would be prepared to pay to avoid the noise. One way would be simply to ask them. But if there is no prospect of actually having to pay anything people will tend to overstate the monetary value of their inconvenience. A more objective method is to establish the cost of sound-proofing. In principle this should enable an upper limit to the 'marginal cost of noise' to be calculated. Sound-proofing will be essential for schools, hospitals, etc., within the noise contours of a new airport. Unfortunately it is difficult to insulate a house only partially; it tends to be an all-or-none job. And for the noise-hater it underestimates the nuisance as it takes no account of noise experienced in the garden or in the streets.

Another, and more subtle, method is to investigate property values. In principle these will take account of all the costs and benefits of living in a house, including fabric, neighbourhood and noise. If the general level of house prices in an area falls as noise levels increase, this fall can be taken as a measure of the monetary loss due to the noise increase. A practical snag is that other factors will alter at the same time (such as job availability) so a multiple regression analysis would be necessary to discover how much of the change was due to extra noise. But even the fall in house prices is not the whole story. To this must be added the expenses of removal for those who actually sell and go elsewhere and the fall in the consumers' surpluses of those who remain. These considerations apply just as much to road as to aircraft noise. Most work to date has concentrated on the 'choice of technique' problem of which types of noise barrier are the more effective. Roadside barriers seem to be far more effective than wide strips of land between the road and property; roads in cuttings are more effective than raised roads, and so on. But the different and more difficult question of how far to go in noise reduction cannot be solved by cost-benefit analysis without a prior solution of the valuation problems described above.

Congestion

The economic effects of traffic congestion have been fairly thoroughly investigated and the policy implications are of immense importance.[1] The starting point of the analysis is that in peak travel periods an extra vehicle will tend to reduce the rate of traffic flow thus increasing the journey times of all other vehicles. There will be a divergence between the marginal private cost of the extra journey (cost of petrol, wear and tear, time, to the driver) and the marginal social cost (everybody's extra petrol, etc.). Given the capacity of the roads there will be an inverse relationship between the number of vehicles wishing to pass along a route per hour and the speed of travel; this is a technical question. The valuation of consequent cost increases is an economic one. Higher average traffic speeds in towns (e.g., from 10–15 m.p.h.) would certainly yield economic benefits. Estimates of the 'saving' that would result from raising speeds to, say, 25 m.p.h. by traffic restriction have put it as high as £1000 m. per year. Starting from the basic premise that reduced congestion would be beneficial, I wish to look at three important policy implications.

1. Existing road space should be rationed by means of 'road-pricing'. One writer has suggested that a 30p per hour charge in Central London might yield a net benefit of £5–6 m. a year. Of course, pricing is not the only, nor the most obvious way of rationing road space; direct prohibition of certain types of vehicle is much simpler and much cheaper to implement. But it is nothing like as flexible as a pricing system could be. A trader or a private

---

1 *Road Pricing: The Economic and Technical Possibilities* (the Smeed report), H.M.S.O., 1964; and *Better Use of Town Roads*, H.M.S.O., 1967.

motorist who really wished to travel during the peak would be free to do so—at a price. If persistent peak travel puts a trader's costs up and affects his prices, this is as it should be. His consumers would merely be paying for resources which they had previously enjoyed for nothing. Road pricing is flexible too, in that it could be varied by time of day and by district as traffic volumes warranted. The main costs and benefits can be set out as in the table.

Costs	Benefits
Extra costs to 'diverted' traffic	Reduced costs to car and lorry users
Costs of the pricing scheme itself	Reduced costs to public transport

While the costs of implementing direct physical restriction would be less, so also would the benefits. Technical studies have shown that road pricing is feasible. I would argue that the usual criticisms of price mechanisms (see Chapter 4) have less force than usual in this case. In their choice of travel 'mode' for routine journeys to work, people behave in a fairly rational way and it is reasonable to assume that they know what is good for them (in contrast to education and health). Secondly, the redistributive results do not look particularly undesirable, though this would depend partly on how the revenue thus raised was spent.

2. No matter which form of restriction was adopted, there would be implications for investment policy. At lower levels of congestion, much of the road investment now undertaken on a jam-busting basis would have to be reconsidered.

3. Traffic and urban planning cannot be considered separately from one another. When alternative types of development are being considered for an urban site one of the most important considerations is the present value of the annual rentals which the new development is expected to command. The difference between this amount and the actual costs of development represents the apparent net monetary benefit (and may be divided between the developer and the local authority). Now cost-benefit analysts can take this only as a starting

point. The particular modification to be mentioned here concerns congestion costs. Some types of development, particularly office blocks, generate far greater traffic volumes than others. Congestion costs, on the basis already discussed, can be measured in, say, £'s per annum per thousand square feet of floor space. Having been reduced to present value, the cost can be subtracted from the net benefit as conventionally calculated. There is evidence that an allowance for congestion costs can alter the ranking of various projects quite dramatically. The reader is reminded that this is merely one instance of a general proposition; that traffic schemes, development plans, urban renewal projects, etc., must as far as possible to considered as a whole. Only then are all the costs and benefits likely to be measured.

Recreation

To clear up rivers so that fishing and bathing once again become possible, to preserve an area of great beauty as a national park, to allow some sailing on water reservoirs, are all considered to be 'good things' from the community's point of view. Is there any measure of the benefits derived, a measure that will enable one to compare 'recreational' projects with one another? On the whole I believe it is undesirable to measure the benefits of a recreational project in terms of what people would be prepared to pay. A crude way of doing this (as in some of the American literature) would be to discover how many people use the facility per day and multiply up by the money worth of each day's enjoyment. There is the fundamental objection of market orientation, apart from any question of feasibility. Having said this, there have been a few very worthwhile technical studies of the value people seem to attach to existing recreational centres (particularly fisheries). The analysis is based on the empirical observation that the number of visitors to a recreational centre (*ceteris paribus*) tends to fall off as distance increases. On certain assumptions about travel and time costs, an inverse relationship can be established between the cost of getting to the centre and the number of visitors. Making the further assumption that people look upon entrance fees in the same kind of way as other expenditure, it is possible to derive a demand curve for the recreational centre itself. The area under the demand curve is consumers' surplus, and this decreases as the entrance fee is raised. If the entrance fee (most commonly zero) is known, total benefit can therefore be derived.

Many kinds of recreational problem are far less tractable. I mention only three here:

(1) Decisions about investment in *new* facilities (as opposed to evaluating existing facilities) require forecasts of future demand. This reservation should not be pressed too far, however, for it is in some measure true of all investment decisions.

(2) Public open space in city centres is highly desirable. But how much value can be put on an acre of public open space as against an acre of offices or factories?

(3) Many of the really big decisions are about *conservation* rather than the provision of new facilities. How much is it worth to keep the Lake District National Park free of property development?

No analyst has the answers to these (yet!). One method is to examine the actual past behaviour of planners in various situations. Their preferences, or trade-offs between one use and another, will reveal themselves in past decisions. One should, however, be quite clear as to what one is trying to achieve; one should distinguish between a positive analysis that will predict the actions of planners in various situations, and a normative analysis which says how planners ought to behave.

Assessment

CB is still in a relatively early stage of development. Its advantages are very considerable: pressure to consider alternative projects, encouragement to list all externalities, consistency in the use of value judgements and so on. But there are also disadvantages. One of these is in the treatment of 'intangibles'. Admittedly they should be listed along with those measured in money, but the absence of a hard cash figure could well put those schemes rich in intangible advantages in a less favourable position than under more old-fashioned methods of assessment.

Secondly, there are technical difficulties in relying on market or pseudo-market valuations. We have already noticed that shadow prices may be more important than actual market prices when these do not adequately reflect opportunity cost. Similarly, inputs purchased or outputs sold at monopoly prices will be wrongly valued from the efficiency standpoint. Further, a very big investment project will have major effects on both input and output prices; for this reason it is commonly said that CB has to be restricted to 'small' projects. And in countries whose market sector is very small the analysis will, *a fortiori*, be inapplicable.

Thirdly, the use of market values, actual or implicit, raises all the normative difficulties associated with free markets, principally income distribution and consumer sovereignty. Nevertheless, as long as CB is applied critically, with a due awareness of its normative connotations, its net effect must be to improve decision-making in the public sector.

10 SECOND-BEST

The approaches to policy discussed in the last three chapters are, in an important sense, 'piecemeal'. They suggest that if we apply certain rules to individual projects or individual sectors we can be sure of securing potential improvements (or increases in real income). To recapitulate, these rules were:

Chapter 7: Intervene in the private sector, or in decentralised parts of the public sector, to ensure that each activity is pursued to the level at which marginal social costs and benefits are equal to one another.

Chapter 8: Ensure that in the public sector prices are set so as to equal marginal cost of production (except at full capacity), and invest in new plant whenever net present value exceeds zero.

Chapter 9: Apply cost-benefit analysis to public sector projects where appropriate.

To understand the second-best objection to piecemeal policies we need to understand the nature of first-best. As we saw in Chapter 2, the basic data of an economic system are

| preferences | production functions | resources |

The rules discussed in Chapters 2 and 4 for an efficient allocation of resources were essentially the mathematical conditions for maximising some preference function, subject to production functions and resources. They consist in a familiar set of marginal (or first-order) conditions.

Now suppose that apart from these very basic constraints there is the further constraint of 'deviant' behaviour in some part of the system. That is to say, there is a 'distortion' such that the appropriate marginal condition does not hold: for example, monopolistic behaviour, the existence of a tariff or a subsidy. There must then be an entirely new set of rules for the efficient allocation of resources.

There will be a new set of marginal (or first-order) conditions. But the three rules given above implicitly assume a first-best situation.

The theory of second-best makes the point that these rules might not be any good when other constraints or 'distortions' are present (for example, export subsidies, monopolies, taxes at the margin). There is no *general* way of knowing whether one makes the situation better or worse by applying a first-best rule in a *second-best* situation. There will, however, be a second-best optimum which can, in principle, be discovered. A second-best model will be just like a first-best model except that a number of behavioural constraints (distortions) have to be added. The rules for optimality emerging from the model are likely to be very much more complex than the simple rules of first-best.

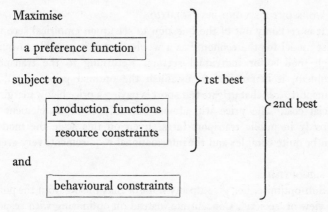

Consider the proposition that coal should be sold at a price equal to its marginal cost of production (suitably defined). From an efficiency standpoint this can be shown to be a desirable policy. But now suppose that a competing fuel, say oil, is being sold at a price considerably above marginal cost *and that this distortion cannot be removed*. The first-best pricing rule will lead to too much coal and too little oil being used. A second-best rule for coal pricing is then needed.

The implications of this theory for a so-called 'piecemeal' economic policy are very serious indeed and seem to call for pessimism, or at least agnosticism. We can have confidence in no proposed policy measure unless it is worked out on a fully second-best basis; but we simply do not have the information to be able to carry out such a vast general equilibrium second-best exercise. All we can do in this chapter is to sketch a number of reactions to the existence of the problem.

1. IGNORE IT

This is by far the most common response. One continues to advocate policies like marginal cost pricing in the hope that no one will raise the embarrassing question, or that for practical purposes it does not matter. One leaves the problem to theorists while practical men get on with their work.

2. WORK OUT A SECOND-BEST SOLUTION

It is certainly out of the question to set up an empirical second-best model for the economy as a whole. But it is possible to build such models for individual sectors. Returning to the transport problem, it is possible to establish the optimal price of public transport *given* that private transport is paying a price below marginal social cost. The price will almost certainly allow an element of subsidy in public transport fares. Even on this scale the models can be quite complex and the informational requirements very great.

3. SUB-OPTIMISE

Sub-optimise, i.e., give up any hope of maximising from the point of view of 'society'. Concentrate instead on optimising with respect to a particular sector. Thus, managers in the electricity industry are set certain goals (expand at such and such a rate, achieve at least a target rate of return); their efforts should be devoted to meeting these. Let policy makers (and welfare economists!) worry about the economy as a whole. This approach has been characterised by one writer as 'third-best'.[1] It is not, by the way, identical with reaction 1. For one thing its rationale is more sophisticated. For

---

1   R. Turvey, 'Present Value versus Internal Rate of Return—An Essay in the Theory of Third-best', *Economic Journal*, March, 1963.

another it feels no obligation to follow traditional first-best policies. It can, of course, incorporate the second solution within its sub-optimisation exercise. The trouble with this reaction is that while it is perfectly understandable from the standpoint of managers and those who have to advise them, it is not very helpful to the policy maker who has to set the goals.

4. FIND THE CONDITIONS FOR A PIECEMEAL SOLUTION

While fully accepting the general theory of second-best, some writers have tried to establish the conditions under which the second-best and first-best rules would turn out to be the same. Where this is so, it will be possible to use the first-best rules directly. It appears (though its relevance is still controversial) that second-best and first-best rules will diverge from one another only when 'externalities' (see Chapter 7) are present. In all other cases the market is able to take distortions into account. The commonsense of this is that one should not worry too much about *distant* distortions; an imperfection in the jam market should not constitute a ground for revising one's rules about the price of steel. Exponents of piecemeal policy have then to show that their policy sector is not (to any appreciable degree) linked with a distorted sector. The larger the policy sector and the greater the number of distortions the less likely are first-best policies to be appropriate.

5. ACT ON THE CONSTRAINT ITSELF

Strictly speaking (in terms of theory) this is cheating, for the theory of second-best assumes that nothing can be done about the be-havioural constraint (or the deviation or distortion). But in terms of policy there is no reason at all why one should make this assumption, and many real world measures of piecemeal policy do attempt to 'remove' or 'correct' the deviation. This is the rationale of anti-monopoly policy and of non-tariff harmonisation in internal trade. Removal of any constraint must, of course, leave the solution un-affected at the very least and will probably improve it. A similar, but less direct, method would be to act on the constraint by imposing corrective taxes and subsidies. Thus in the urban transport case already mentioned, an alternative to working out a second-best

PIECEMEAL RULES

public transport fare would be to impose road pricing in the private
sector and then follow a first-best public transport solution.

These five types of reaction present between them a confused
picture. On the whole, practising economists are much less disturbed
by second-best than, on the face of it, they ought to be. Perhaps
their instinct is sound, but the burden of proof that second-best
can be set safely to one side lies squarely on the economic adviser.

11 PRICES AND PLANNING

The policies considered in the last three chapters are piecemeal policies in rather a special sense; they are applied to one part, the public sector, of an economy that remains basically a market economy. These rules are themselves based upon the well-known conditions for efficient production and exchange normally associated with 'competition'. The chapter on second-best showed that the pursuit of such rules can be argued to bring maximum efficiency, let alone social welfare, in only a rough and ready way.

Many of the objections to these rules collapse, however, when they are *universally* applied within an economy. If there are distortions, the planner is presumably free to remove them.

The ideal decentralised planning procedure is then as follows:

(1) The planners, on the basis of their own preferences and value judgements, set relative weights or valuations on commodities for final consumption.

(2) Given the technology and a knowledge of the basic resource constraints, they are able to calculate imputed or shadow prices in a manner to be explained below. These factor prices should, of course, be set to include external costs and benefits in the sense discussed in Chapter 9.

(3) Individual enterprises are then faced with given output and factor prices and enjoined to adjust output so that price equals marginal cost. Similarly, they are enjoined to increase capacity whenever the net present value of doing so exceeds zero.

We see in Chapter 13 that this process comes rather near the market socialist solution to pricing (discussed a great deal by western economists in the 1930s). The traditional Soviet material balances approach—also to be explained below—provides very little scope for the use of prices in anything but an administrative sense.

The rest of this section is devoted to a simple verbal exposition of the meaning and uses of linear programming and a numerical example, solved graphically, is provided in the appendix at the end of the chapter.

It was explained in Chapter 2 that a great many problems of economic behaviour can be handled in terms of constrained optimisation (maximising or minimising something subject to certain constraints). One may treat the behaviour of individuals, business firms or of whole economies in this fashion. As traditionally set up by economists, these constrained maximisation problems are extremely general in form and, except for grossly simplified models (for example, the Cobb-Douglas production function), are very difficult to quantify. They fail to be operationally useful.

Linear programming, on the other hand, is a method of solving a rather less general but far more tractable form of constrained optimisation problem. We are concerned with firstly, a linear objective function, secondly, a linear technology and thirdly, a set of constraints.

1. The linear objective function is the thing to be maximised or minimised. Each component is simply given a 'weight'. Thus in the appendix example the weights are 4, 3 and 2. In the planning context these weights will reflect the relative importance attached by planners to the various goods to be produced. In the context of the business firm they will reflect the unit profit to be earned on each type of output for sale (or the unit cost of inputs if the aim is cost minimisation.) Clearly it is 'unrealistic' to assume that a weight will be independent of the proportions in which its various components occur. In ordinary consumer theory we assumed that marginal demand price was falling, i.e., that as less food and more clothing became available, the marginal valuation attached to clothing, relative to that attached to food, would fall. Nevertheless, for a wide range of problems a linear objective function is a useful approximation to the planners' or the decision-makers' preferences.

2. The technology implied by the linear programming formulation is very simple. The components of the objective function (outputs) can be achieved by a number of processes or activities such that a unit of the activity calls for certain definite inputs. To find out how many units of input are required for any stated level of the activity, one simply multiplies up in a proportional fashion.

Again, this is only a useful approximation but it lends itself easily to quantification.

3. Constraints on production are given by the linear technology together with limitations on the levels to which the various activities may be pursued. Limitations will often be due to fixed quantities of certain inputs being available.

Quite complex linear programming problems, involving large numbers of variables and constraints can be handled as a matter of routine by modern techniques. But we are not here concerned as much with technique as with economic meaning.

The aspect of linear programming which is of interest to us in this part of the book is as follows. There corresponds to each 'primal' linear programming problem a 'dual' problem; the dual may or may not be of economic interest but it is always there. Consider the overall planning problem. The primal problem is to maximise a weighted sum of output of goods subject to a linear technology and some physical constraints; some resources will be fixed in quantity. Because of the weights, the objective function will be in 'value' terms and is a measure of benefits or receipts (or, in the case of a business firm, profits). The dual looks at the problem, as it were, from the other end. Suppose that all the receipts have to be 'imputed' to those resources which are fixed, that total resource costs have to be minimised and that the price of each output has to equal its costs of production. There will be a set of 'imputed', 'shadow' or 'dual' resource prices which just meet these conditions. They emerge (see appendix) as the solution to a problem that is dual to the primal problem originally posed. Clearly any resource which is not fully used should have a zero shadow price, i.e., none of the total receipts or benefits can be imputed to it.

It was stated in Chapter 2 that under competitive conditions the price of a factor service tends to be equal to its marginal value product. The same notion is relevant to shadow prices. A shadow price shows the amount by which the objective function in the primal problem would be increased as a result of increasing the resource by one unit.

For planning purposes, shadow prices are potentially useful as tools of efficient decentralisation. Consider a large enterprise having a given amount of financial resources. It can calculate a shadow price of financial resources for the organisation as a whole (perhaps expressed as a rate of interest or return). Now suppose that its operations are decentralised. If each plant manager has to pay for financial resources at the shadow price he will never find it worthwhile to embark upon projects that are inefficient from the point of view of the organisation as a whole. The use of shadow prices reconciles efficiency with freedom. To change the context slightly we might imagine a water resource authority delegating its decisions to river managers or, to change the context more drastically, a poor country allocating foreign exchange. The shadow price concept is therefore a very versatile one.

A simple linear programming approach of the kind just outlined will rarely be used just as it stands. For one thing, the costs of obtaining all the relevant information can be high; for another, the attaching of constant 'weights' to outputs might be unrealistic in which case the more complex method of non-linear programming is required. An alternative method is this: start with arbitrary shadow prices; collect bids from each manager for units of the resource at these prices; if demand and supply are unequal, adjust price until they balance; allocate the resource accordingly. Where it is expected that (for various reasons) managers will not be very good at playing this game the initial guesses will have to be fairly close to the 'true' shadow price. In this case, a crude linear programme could be useful to determine the rough orders of magnitude of the shadow prices.

Linear programming and more complex techniques built upon it are of obvious importance to any attempt to use prices simply as a means of efficient decentralisation. If the planners have done their sums properly, individual plants and households will be led, as it were, by an invisible hand to fulfill planners' preferences. Competitive equilibrium is then seen to be rather a special case in that,

(1) Shadow prices (alias marginal value products) are actually paid to individuals who own factor services.
(2) This determines the incomes of individuals in the system and consequently the weight given to their various preferences in the market place.

PRICES AND PLANNING

Once this link is severed, it can be seen that prices are not necessarily associated with capitalism or with market economies; they are the logical corollaries of any solution to the economic problem.

One of the technical snags preventing a free market from reaching competitive equilibrium was the prevalence of monopoly or imperfect competition (see Chapter 4). Under a regime of 'weights-plus-shadow-prices', it is presumed that 'the state' decides on the weights and the shadow prices are derived from a programming exercise. Individual business firms must take them as given, so that they therefore play the same kind of rôle as under perfect competition. It will often be convenient, however, to use actual markets as a device for approximating to the programming prices (there will then, however, be scope for the use of monopoly power whenever it arises). Externalities were another technical snag and these too can, in principle, easily be taken into account; so long as external effects enter into the preferences of the planner and so long as he assigns a non-zero weight to them, they must react upon the prevailing shadow prices and prices.

The increasing returns snag is not so easily overcome. We have already seen that if the prices of inputs and outputs are given there will be no equilibrium level of output for the firm experiencing increasing returns. This means that some kind of positive central intervention will be necessary. Individual plants will have to be given explicit instructions about the quantities of inputs and outputs to be used.

Appendix

I. A PRIMAL PROBLEM

Three types of goods are to be produced: x_1, x_2, and x_3

Let the planner attach weights of 4, 3 and 2 to units of these goods

Let there be 12 units of resource y_1 available and
12 units of resource y_2

Let the production of 1 unit of x_1 use 1 unit of y_1 and 4 units of y_2

,, ,, ,, ,, ,, ,, ,, x_2 use 1 unit of y_1 and $\frac{3}{2}$ units of y_2

,, ,, ,, ,, ,, ,, ,, x_3 use 1 unit of y_1 and $\frac{1}{2}$ units of y_2

The problem can then be set out as follows:

Maximise $4x_1 + 3x_2 + 2x_3$ (R)

Subject to the constraints

$$x_1 + x_2 + x_3 \leqslant 12$$
and $\quad 4x_1 + \tfrac{3}{2}x_2 + \tfrac{1}{2}x_3 \leqslant 12$

and that none of these quantities is negative.

2. THE DUAL PROBLEM

Let P_1 be the imputed price of y_1 and

P_2 ,,   ,,   ,,   ,,   ,, y_2

The dual problem is

Minimise $\quad 12P_1 + 12P_2$ (C)

Subject to the constraints

$$P_1 + 4P_2 \geqslant 4$$
$$P_1 + \tfrac{3}{2}P_2 \geqslant 3$$
$$P_1 + \tfrac{1}{2}P_2 \geqslant 2$$

and that none of these prices is negative.

The three constraints state that the imputed cost of production of each good must not be less than its price.

Notice a marked symmetry between the primal and dual. The same numbers appear on the left hand side of the constraints in each case, but they are re-arranged to read vertically now instead of horizontally. Further, the constraints in the one problem appear in the objective function of the other. In the dual, the inequalities are reversed and the objective function is to be minimised, not maximised.

3. THE SOLUTION

It is easiest, in this case, to approach the solution graphically via the dual. In Figure 8 the three heavy lines represent the three constraints and the other line represents the objective function. All the points to the north-east of the constraint are feasible but there

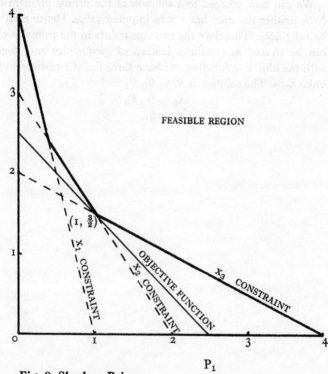

Fig. 8. Shadow Prices

is only one optimal solution. Notice that the objective function (C) has been drawn at $45°$ to the axes because we assumed equal quantities of the two resources y_1 and y_2. The lowest obtainable value of (C) will be where $P_1 = 1$ and $P_2 = \frac{3}{2}$.

These are the shadow or dual prices we have been seeking. Now that we have the shadow prices the value of (C) can easily be seen to be 30. But as all value has been imputed to the two resources it must be the case that (at solution values) the maximum value of the objective function (R) must equal (C).

Hence $\qquad\qquad R = C = 30.$

PIECEMEAL RULES

We can now proceed to a solution of the primal problem itself. Now neither resource has a zero imputed value. Hence each must be fully used. Therefore the two constraints in the primal problem can be treated as equalities instead of inequalities and, together with the objective function, we have three linear equations to three unknowns. The solution is $x_1 = 0$ $P_1 = 1$

$$x_2 = 6 \quad P_2 = \tfrac{3}{2}$$
$$x_3 = 6.$$

PART III

POLICY

12 POLICY AND THE MARKET

The market place is a thing not to be revered or despised but to be used. It is attractive as a decentralised device for taking decisions in a more or less efficient way; but it is repulsive in that it ignores wider social objectives and, when left alone, develops unpleasant monopoly characteristics.

The general theme of this last section is that provided one takes sufficient care, prices and markets can be useful instruments in reaching targets of policy. A brief summary follows of how this general theme is treated in each of the remaining chapters.

CHAPTER 13

The clumsiness of administrative planning is seen as a good reason for Eastern European and Soviet experiments in greater decentralisation of economic power. Thus the allowing of more discretion to enterprising managers and more reliance on the market. This policy seems to have its dangers for precisely the same sorts of reason as in Chapter 4.

CHAPTER 14

Big business is sufficiently sheltered from the compulsion to maximise profits that managers are alleged to be free to turn to other pursuits. This, added to the relative inefficiency of the takeover mechanism, suggests that the structure of industry as thrown up by market processes is to some extent arbitrary. It is argued that this justifies positive intervention of the kind practised, until recently, by the I.R.C.

CHAPTER 15

Social services involve goods or services that *either* imply income redistribution *or* are particularly important goods or services (like education, health) *or* are public goods of a kind provided for all. Liberal economists have long argued that the market process is not an adequate means of resource allocation in this area.

POLICY

CHAPTER 16

The private housing markets in the U.K. (including private renting and owner-occupation) are important not only directly, but because a full understanding of how they work is necessary to the implementation of policies for 'improving' the housing situation. Simple economic policy rules, like cost minimisation can be useful, provided that policy-makers remain aware of value judgements underlying apparently objective data.

CHAPTER 17

'Free trade' and free international mobility of factors are the appropriate policy rules for maximising real income. But there may be all sorts of reasons, from protection of vulnerable groups at home to discriminatory policies in favour of developing countries, why a country might reasonably wish to adopt other policies.

CHAPTER 18

The free market is liable to throw up a special type of casualty when labour-saving technical progress is rapid. Special measures are required to minimise the hardship this causes to individuals.

114

13 PRICES IN SOCIALIST COUNTRIES

The problem

Prices played a fairly limited part in Soviet and Eastern European economic planning up to the late 1950s. Since then, there has been a lot of discussion about the rôle of prices and markets within the context of socialist planning, particularly in Poland, Hungary and Czechoslovakia. There has also been a more modest debate within the Soviet Union centering upon the celebrated Liberman proposals dating from 1962. The basic issue is about decentralisation. How far is it possible not only to allow more freedom to individual plant managers but also to allow prices (including perhaps wage-rates and the rate of interest) to be determined by market forces? This is only partly a question of economic techniques. Even more important, it is a question of power. A basic assumption of those who oppose reform is that decentralisation means loss of control by the party. On the whole they are probably right. Under the system of physical planning (Tonnen-ideologie) the central organisation exercised detailed control over individual enterprises. Further, the task of the manager was to implement certain directives whose fulfilment could be measured in terms of a number of simple indices. The new type of manager is likely to be a greater danger to the party. Some of the reformers have, however, argued persuasively that a few simple economic levers (interest and credit policy for example) could be far more effective in attaining the objectives of the centre than a massive flow of more or less useless information.

One must remember that despite all the discussion, the actual use of markets as western readers know them is extremely limited. Even where quite drastic reforms have been implemented, the custom has been to have several categories of price such that only a small proportion of goods is really subject to the free market. Most notably, the prices of basic food and materials are fixed almost universally by the central authorities; the goods subject to market forces tend to be those consumer goods whose supply and demand position is roughly in balance.

POLICY

I shall use this chapter as an opportunity to introduce the technique of input-output analysis. This should not be taken to mean that it is relevant only to socialist planning: it is, in fact, of extremely wide application.

Historical sketch

For the first year or so after the Revolution of 1917 Lenin operated a policy of 'War Communism' but frankly confessed failure, turning by 1921 to the New Economic Policy (NEP) whose leading theoretical apologist was Bukharin. The chief motive for NEP was the state of Soviet agriculture; the peasants would have to be attracted into the Soviet system on favourable terms of trade instead of being coerced, 'We have', said Lenin, 'to tell the whole peasantry . . . get rich, accumulate, develop your economy'. Discussion then shifted to the balance between investment and consumption and between industry and agriculture, the practical problem being that excess industrial capital, available after the war years, was not fully utilised. Middle of the road writers argued that quick returns could be had by investment in labour-intensive sectors (light industry and agriculture). At this stage Preobrazhensky,[1] the theorist of Trotskyist opposition, forcibly argued that very large increases in industrial investment were necessary to prevent further shortages of goods, and that labour for heavy industry could be obtained from potential labour surpluses in agriculture. He drew an analogy with Marx's analysis of 'primitive capitalistic accumulation'.

The price policy of NEP was to be abandoned. Instead of offering favourable terms of trade to the peasants, the state would take advantage of its monopoly position as a buyer in order to turn the terms of trade against them. Preobrazhensky referred to this as a suspension of the law of value. Price policy was to be completely subordinate to the process of socialistic accumulation. Stalin at first opposed this line of argument, pressing instead for the moderate

---

1 E. Preobrazhensky (trans. by B. Pearce), *The New Economics*, London, 1966.

policy of investing in light industry. But, as is now well-known, after the expulsion of Trotsky and Preobrazhensky, Stalin reversed his attitude, not only adopting the policy of industrialisation but pushing it to extremes. Growth of the heavy industrial sector was fed by forced saving and forced collectivisation in agriculture. The over-riding objective of growth meant that other problems of resource allocation and especially 'consumer choice' were of little importance. The era of the five year plans had started. The main planning tool was the device of 'material balances', the theoretical basis for which will be explained in the next section.

For the first decade or so after the Second World War, the balances approach, with its emphasis on growth, was followed by the Eastern European bloc. Discussion of a more liberal economic policy became possible only when the process of de-Stalinisation had begun, and became relevant only when the most urgent problems of growth had been solved. It was stimulated by continuing shortages of consumer goods. The Yugoslavs (having broken with Stalin in 1947) were the first to experiment, but by the mid fifties the Poles, under Gomulka, proposed an ambitious new economic model for quasi-market conditions; similar discussions took place under Kadar in Hungary. But this first wave of reform discussions was premature and its practical effects negligible.

The second, more important, wave of economic revisionism came in the early sixties, mainly as a consequence of economic crises, particularly in agriculture. Compared with some of the other countries the Polish contribution was by this time fairly conservative. Decentralisation and profit were accepted, but central control over prices maintained. The Soviet discussion, following Liberman's proposals for greater use of bonuses at the enterprise level, led to Kosygin's report of 1965. But this discussion was again conservative for Liberman accepted central control of prices *and* output targets leaving managers free only in their selection of inputs, choice of quality and so on. Under Kosygin's proposals enterprises still have to accept a given 'wages fund' but receive credits instead of grants for investment purposes. At the other extreme the Yugoslavs are moving very firmly in the direction of a completely free market; this retains its essential link with socialism by means of workers' councils which make the crucial decisions at the local level. They suffered from acute inflation, falls in real wages and some unemployment after the 1965 reforms, though this was partly alleviated by emigration.

Between these extremes the Eastern Germans, the Hungarians and the Czechs have gone quite a long way since 1965. They have all introduced the system of price 'categories'. Implementation was slow in Czechoslovakia under Novodny, especially as the reforms seemed to produce inflation, but much more was done under Dubcek up to the invasion of 1968. The Hungarians were unique in 1968 in that they reformed wholesale and retail prices in one go. Finally, there has been a substantial shift to private farming in Poland and in Yugoslavia.

There has therefore been a major shift towards decentralised routine economic decision-making accompanied by greater use of free markets, private ownership and the profit motive. The spectrum of change has Russia, cautiously experimenting in the use of inputs by enterprises, and Yugoslavia, with its wide use of free markets, at its extremes.

Theory and policy

Parallel with the Soviet developments of the 1920s and 1930s ran a discussion among some western theorists about the possibility of a rational socialism. The anti-socialist argument, presented mainly by von Mises and Hayek, was that rational calculation would be impossible. The reason for this was that producers would have no scientific way of telling efficient methods of production from inefficient ones. The 'best' combination of labour, materials and capital is given not by technological considerations alone but by technology together with prices. Now there would be no way of determining input prices (particularly the prices of capital goods) without markets, and no markets without private ownership. Socialism was not impossible; it was just inefficient. There is some force in this. The Soviet Union has always had difficulty in fixing the prices of producer goods (group A goods) and in settling the prices at which goods were to be exchanged as between state enterprises. Without a market, or a pseudo-market, there could be no solution.

In the early 'thirties the discussion was carried a great deal further by Lange, Lerner and Dickinson who suggested a series of devices known as 'market socialism'. Their starting point was Pareto's demonstration of the efficiency of competition; their central contribution was that a socialist system could behave *as if* markets were operating. In principle it would be possible to assemble information about what the supply and demand schedules would be *if* markets existed, and to use computers for working out an equilibrium set of prices for the whole system. But this would be costly and impracticable. The alternative was to set prices by trial and error. If a price was too high or too low symptoms of excess supply or demand could be observed and the price adjusted. Assuming that markets were stable this would lead to a whole set of equilibrium prices. Individual enterprises would be given quite simple 'rules' to follow. These could be represented as the double condition:

—adjust output so that marginal cost equals price
—adjust input so that marginal value product equals price.

The central authority would then have the task of adjusting both commodity and input prices until market supply equalled market demand. A system of this kind would have major advantages over free market capitalism, not least of which would be the absence of monopoly. Dickinson pushed the argument a little further to suggest that *real* markets could be used, even in the determination of interest rates. This would not, he argued, be incompatible with socialism so long as something was done at the same time to make the distribution of income equitable and to safeguard the production of those goods too important to be left to market forces. Dickinson's position was substantially the same as that now taken by many of the Eastern European reformers.

A final rebuttal of von Mises had to wait upon the use of linear programming techniques.[1] Consider an economy in which the basic resources are fixed but not privately owned, i.e., there is no

---

[1]   L. V. Kantorovich (trans. by P. F. Knightsfield), *Best Use of Economic Resources*, London, 1964.

actual market in basic resources. Suppose that a number of final goods is to be produced whose values are known (they may simply be values assigned by the planners). Suppose also that there is a linear relationship between each good and the quantity of each resource needed to manufacture it; this can be shown as a set of 'fixed coefficients'. The obvious economic problem is to produce the largest valuation of goods possible given the various resource constraints. This is a problem in linear programming (the so-called 'primal' problem) and, if the information is available, can be solved by the use of computers. The important thing from our point of view is that the solution of the 'primal' problem implies the solution of another, 'dual', problem. Just as the primal solution is a set of outputs, the dual solution will be a set of 'shadow' or 'dual' prices. These are approximations to the marginal value products of the fixed resources; Kantorovich named them 'objectively determined valuations' to contrast them with the arbitrary nature of input prices as actually used in planning (see Chapter 11).

The use of programming provides, in principle, an enormous simplification of central control. The planners would be quite free to put whatever valuations they wish upon final products. They would establish the resources available and the set of technical coefficients, a computer programme would calculate the appropriate shadow prices which could then be the actual prices charged to firms for use of resources. Three things are simultaneously achieved:

(1) Planners, together with politicians, make the key policy decisions about output.
(2) Planners establish shadow prices on a scientific basis.
(3) Individual managers are given 'freedom' from direct central control.

One drawback is, of course, the practical one of handling large volumes of information and a large number of computations. There are other, more fundamental, drawbacks but as these are common to all types of market socialism they are deferred to the end of this section.

The economic device which these various forms of market socialism are intended to replace is the standard system of material balances whose theoretical counterpart is input-output analysis. Essentially, this is very simple indeed. The planners consider some 'menu' of goods (usually last year's menu with some changes). Given the technical relationships of the system, the production function, they are able to calculate what the resource requirements will be. If spare capacity is then available the 'menu' can be increased; if capacity is short either the menu can be reduced or extra resources somehow squeezed out. This last possibility is especially useful if firms are suspected of using highly inefficient methods. The process is continued until a rough balance is attained. Such an exercise is usually part of a five or seven year plan but is sometimes not completed until the second or third year of the plan. It is then possible to send detailed instructions to firms as to what their output will be. Each manager can be told which outputs to produce and which inputs to use; there is no room for prices except as a purely accounting device. A very simple material balance exercise is shown below. Let there be two industries A and B and one primary input, labour, L. For every unit of A produced, $\frac{2}{5}$ of a unit of A, $\frac{1}{4}$ of a unit of B, etc., will be used up in its production as in Table 1.

	A	B
A	$\frac{2}{5}$	$\frac{1}{10}$
B	$\frac{1}{4}$	$\frac{1}{5}$
L	$\frac{1}{10}$	$\frac{1}{5}$

Table 1. Table of coefficients

Suppose that 50 units of labour is the total available. Then a material balance that uses up all the labour is shown below.

	A	B	Final output	Total output
A	40	20	40	100
B	25	40	135	200
L	10	40	—	—

Table 2. A material balance

Thus 200 units of B can be produced altogether, 135 of which go to final consumers, 25 as input to industry A and 40 to industry B. If there were 10 firms in industry B the following instruction could go out to the manager of each, 'Make 20 units of B. Use in its production 2 units of A, 4 of B and 4 of labour.'

Notice that one or two elementary forms of incentive are possible even with this system. There can be penalties for falling short of the 'norm' for output or exceeding 'norms' for inputs, and rewards (medals or whatever) for exceeding output norms or undershooting input norms. But there is no need for the firm to have to buy the material inputs or its labour.

There are many other material balances possible apart from the one shown in the table; more of A or less of B may be produced given the total resources of labour available. The planners' task is to work out the possible alternatives and then to ask the policy-makers to choose between them.

Discussions of proposals for reform in the Soviet system have largely taken the form of criticising the many absurdities of the material balances system. Its main justification, detailed control by the central party organisation, became less convincing as de-Stalinisation proceeded. The first bunch of criticisms concerns the enormous costs of conveying information up and down the system of control. The technical coefficients, as shown in Table 1, are in fact collected by a process of trial and error. The centre 'tries out' certain menus and asks the enterprises what the resource requirements would be. The replies are then added together and the feasibility of the menu determined. This process usually has to be repeated several times. Once the norms are determined, the enterprise has to make frequent applications for resources and submit frequent records of its output. The system is bureaucratic and highly expensive in terms of information costs. Further, the requests for information are so poorly designed and so inconsistent between enterprises as to be of little use in decision-making. A large part of the effort is therefore useless as well as expensive. Secondly, the setting of norms in physical terms led to poor decisions about the composition of output. This is because it is extremely difficult to think of a simple physical indicator that will achieve what is wanted.

PRICES IN SOCIALIST COUNTRIES

A large fund of 'horror-stories' now exists of 'norms' for nails, wheelbarrows, cooking utensils, and so on, being fixed in terms of weight. The easiest way of earning a bonus is then to produce extremely heavy nails, wheelbarrows and saucepans regardless of whether the consumers want them. This disregard for consumer choice together with a continuing sellers' market in consumer goods led to widespread criticism. Thirdly, resources were often provided 'free' to the enterprise (in the early years the outputs of state enterprises were transferred to one another 'free'). This was particularly so for labour and funds for capital investment. But these practices were among the first to suffer in the reforms of the sixties though it is still common for firms to have a wages-fund; thus labour is free up to the point at which the fund is exhausted.

Taken together, these criticisms made a formidable dent in the old policy. Before reforms could be pushed very far, on the other hand, it would be necessary to have an objective basis for price formation. Let us start from the standard Marxist position that the value of a commodity is given by the value of the 'socially necessary' labour going into it. Because of the five year plan method it is customary to have infrequent price 'reforms' rather than a large number of small changes. If indirect as well as direct labour is included (that is, labour necessary to make machinery) the orthodox values correspond very roughly to what we know as 'costs of production'. An extension of the technical coefficients approach, just outlined, is a suitable tool for periodic recalculation of prices on a cost of production basis. Returning to the simple two industry example and reading *down the columns* it must be the case that

Price of A (per unit) = $\frac{2}{5}$ (price of A) + $\frac{1}{4}$ (price of B) + $\frac{1}{10}$ (price of labour)

Price of B (per unit) = $\frac{1}{10}$ (price of A) + $\frac{1}{5}$ (price of B) + $\frac{1}{5}$ (price of labour)

But this gives two equations for three unknown prices. Let the price of labour, the wage-rate, be fixed at some figure, say unity. Then the approximate prices of the goods are:

Price of A (per unit) = 0·29

Price of B (per unit) = 0·29.

Using these values together with the physical quantities in Table 2, it is possible to draw up a simple social accounting table. Prices have simply been multiplied by quantities.

Sales ╲ purchases	A	B	Final output	Total output
A	11·6	5·8	11·6	29
B	7·3	11·6	39·2	58
L	10·0	40·0	50(50·8)	—
	28·9	57·4	—	87(86·3)

Table 3. Social accounting table

Notice that the value of *all* the sales of an industry must equal the value of all its purchases, and that the value of goods sold to consumers (51) is approximately equal to the wages paid out (50). This slight discrepancy is entirely due to my rounding off during the calculations. If other categories of payment had been included (profits for instance) then wages *plus* profits would equal the value of final output. The figure approximates to the western concept of net national income or product. The gross figure 87(86) is less satisfactory as it counts goods used up during the process of production; it 'double-counts'.

On this basis it is possible to draw up a set of 'values', useful for accounting and other purposes without recourse to the market. But are they useful for economic purposes? Leaving the computational and data collection problems to one side, the concept of 'fixed coefficients' has serious limitations. Look again at Table 1. It implies that for each good only one method of production would ever be chosen. With only one basic input, labour, this will in fact be the case. More generally if other basic payments have to be made, notably profit, it will no longer be possible to say which is the best technique of production without knowing the relative prices of the

124

inputs. If one is using an input-output analysis as part of a general macroeconomic forecasting exercise it is possible to *vary* the coefficients over time on an ad hoc basis; but it is not very useful to do this if the aim of the exercise is to make rational decisions at the industry or firm level.

Even so, we have seen that the material balances method *can* be operated with an objectively determined set of prices, though these are of limited use for economic purposes. And it has the definite advantage over market socialism that 'planners' preferences' are firmly in the saddle. The various sets of final demands tried and the set finally chosen are all generated by the planner, not by the consumer. This gives a useful lever to ensure that basic priorities are being attained. But this very advantage must lead to pressures for change. At the wages being paid and at the cost of production prices charged, people may not wish to buy the set of final outputs chosen by the planners. Many responses to this are possible, depending on the form taken by the imbalance. Firstly people may wish to spend more on consumer goods in total than is currently possible (a situation of repressed inflation). Unless action is taken, the most likely outcome is an accumulation of liquidity (purchasing power) in the hands of the public and, in the end, to serious inflationary pressures. Some form of tax is the obvious solution, either on earnings or on goods. In the Soviet Union the traditional form of tax is a turnover tax. Thus a general increase in the rate of turnover tax could be used to combat inflationary pressures. Secondly, there may be shortages (or excesses) of particular goods, at the cost-of-production prices. The authorities could react to this in several ways; they could raise the output norms of producers (in effect modifying planners' preferences), allow some imports or raise the particular turnover taxes of the goods concerned. But there would be no mechanism whereby an increase in turnover tax (in price) would encourage suppliers to offer more output. This could only be done at the instigation of the centre. If it could be done directly, planners' preferences would be seriously undermined. A 'turnover tax' response to shortages, without adjustments on the supply side, eventually leads to consumer discontent. Notice that the converse response, in the case of excess supply, would be to lower turnover tax; again if this cannot be related to production decisions the excess becomes semi-permanent.

Market socialists want the pattern of production to correspond more closely than in the past to consumer tastes. The Liberman proposals go only a little way in this direction, the Yugoslavs very far indeed. In Poland a number of econometric studies of demand have recently been undertaken. The trend is towards allowing enterprises some control of their own prices (as in the several category price systems). A great danger, as has been pointed out by the Czech economist Sik, is that enterprises will exploit monopoly positions, behaving as profit maximisers. As we saw earlier, competition is an inefficient way of solving the economic problem if monopolistic elements are present. The more enthusiastic marketeers tend to overlook this.

Now consider wages. If individual managers are free to set wages as well as prices and if their own rewards are bonuses based on the amount of profit earned and if monopoly conditions are excluded, there would be a tendency for wage-rates to equal marginal value productivities. The wide range of individual skills and talents makes it most probable that under a more flexible wage system 'differentials' would widen. Those with little skill or intelligence would come out of it rather badly; indeed this is necessary if labour is to be efficiently distributed by means of a price system. It is suggested, therefore, by some of the old guard in Eastern Europe that market socialism must be opposed on grounds of social justice. Unfortunately these objectors ignore the experience of the 1950s, when direction of labour gave way to the judicious use of *planned* wage differentials. Official wage rates were allowed to rise where excess demand symptoms became clear in the labour market. I suggest that the wage-differential problem is not simply about market socialism versus material balances but, more fundamentally, about efficiency versus equality.

Profits, bonuses and so on can be used in a variety of ways as a device for decentralisation. Once a reasonably satisfactory system of prices has been devised, profit can be defined as the difference between receipts and payments for labour and materials, loans, etc. Under a simple system the whole of profit, except for a fixed salary, can be handed over to the central authority, any incentive there is taking the form of exhortation and so on. Any money required for investment purposes is sought from the centre, in grant or loan form. The next simplest form of incentive system is to relate salary to profits by means of 'bonuses', perhaps for workers as well as managers. Extreme decentralisation allows the enterprise to retain all its profits (except for a tax) and to finance its own investments and perhaps those of other enterprises. In the Yugoslav version of worker control, local councils have control over an increasingly large proportion of total profits and make decisions about local social investment (schools, etc.) as well as industrial investment. Once again one has to be very careful about monopoly power—a manager, or even a group of workers, being paid on a profit/bonus system will have every interest in exploiting the consumer. All this makes the role of manager far more interesting and responsible than it has been in the past. Many managers complain that even after the reforms of the sixties they have much less freedom than their western counterparts (though I suspect that many of them have a rose-tinted view of what western managers actually do!). Lastly we must look at the rehabilitation of interest rates. Finance used to be given for investment by means of a central grant. Within the total available, finance was 'free'; there was no interest charge. The reason for this was partly doctrinal and partly practical. Simple versions of a labour theory of value allowed no place for interest rates in the process of price determination. Interest payments constituted the incomes of the old rentier class under capitalism and could play no part in a socialist state. The practical reason was central control over the total volume of investment. Investment could be regarded as just another form of final demand and included in the material balances approach. The use of interest rates to *control* the volume of investment implied loss of direct command. But interest can be viewed as the price of investment funds and an indicator of their scarcity. It gives the individual firm an economic criterion for the choice of production technique, and it gives the centre an indication of the need for funds as between firms and industries. Further, there is no need to have a rentier class and a market for the scientific establishment of interest rates. Given the

127

total volume of funds available, the 'shadow' interest rate can be calculated by linear programming methods already described. The Yugoslavs did, for a short time, experiment with investment determination by means of interest rates through the banks. Firms were asked how much they would like to borrow at various interest rates. Added together, these amounts constituted a demand schedule for funds. At one interest rate demand would equal supply; this would be the equilibrium rate. The experiment (small scale in any case) was dropped after a while largely due to inexperience on the part of banks and firms. Generally the approach to interest rates has been extremely cautious.

The chief theoretical point about interest rates is that *even if* there is no rentier class and *even if* total investment is fixed by the planners, interest rates nevertheless have an important role to play at the microeconomic level. They enable an objective choice between more and less capital intensive projects. A major defect of the old material balance system was that as long as the total costs of two investment projects were the same, the balance between capital and labour was unimportant to the individual manager (so long as the totals came within his budget).

Kantorovich, again, pioneered the use of objectively determined interest rates in the Soviet Union, though subsequent discussion is usually shrouded in obscure terminology due to their controversial nature.

Summary

The traditional method of economic planning in the Soviet bloc is the 'material balance'. The corresponding theoretical tool is input-output analysis. The method enables detailed control by the centre but is costly in terms of information flows and rigid in response to consumer demand. Prices are usually determined in an arbitrary fashion and play a negligible role, particularly in the choice of production techniques. Reforms since the mid-1950s have gradually been moving towards greater use of markets and prices especially for some manufactured consumer goods. Many problems connected with this process have still to be solved. How far should planners' preferences override those of consumers as expressed in the market place? How far should the rate of interest and the volume of investment be determined on a decentralised basis? How can the clash between consideration of efficiency and of equity be resolved? The surprising thing is that these problems are almost universal. They are deep social problems about choice, not peculiar to this or that economic system.

14 BIG BUSINESS

The view taken of big business in this chapter will seem distressingly narrow to sociologists, political scientists and others. It simply asks whether there are any policy tools available for making sure that big business operates in 'the public interest'. General definitions of 'public interest' (the allocation of resources such that social welfare is maximised), unfortunately turn out to be non-operational. The judgement is, in the end, an eclectic one. Are production methods efficient, are innovations encouraged, are profits (or prices) 'unreasonably' high, are scale economies being realised? A fundamental ambivalence towards bigness runs right through economic theory and policy. Forty years ago economists came to accept that their favourite structure (perfect competition) was inconsistent with individual scale economies, that market dominance and efficiency often went hand in hand. Currently, planners are combining traditional anti-monopoly legislation with devices to *encourage* bigness where this can be done without destroying competition. Thus we have the Industrial Reorganisation Corporation in the United Kingdom, the Commissariat du Plan in France, the Instituto per Reconstruzione Industrielo in Italy and the Société Nationale de Crédit à l'Industries (together with the Société Nationale d'Investissements) in Belgium. There are two reasons for this new attitude, one of them (in my opinion) valid and the other invalid. Firstly the merger process has drawn attention to the arbitrary nature of the structure of industry. If the competitive process can be shown not to lead to an optimum structure then a few jolts and prods by the state seem acceptable. Secondly (and less desirably) countries have succumbed to a certain degree of 'mercantilism' in their approach to these problems. They ask not simply what effect a given structure will have on efficiency and competition, but also what effect it will have on the balance of payments. As will be made clearer in Chapter 16, I believe the use of this criterion to be a mistake.

As a backcloth to our discussion we shall need to know something about the structure of a typical manufacturing industry (we pass

BIG BUSINESS

over the problem of defining the term). Three features are of interest to us.

1. THE DISTRIBUTION OF FIRMS IS POSITIVELY SKEWED

When plotted as a graph the size distribution is often approximately 'log-normal', i.e., if plotted in logarithms it would be normal. The most common size of company (the modal size) is smaller than the mean size and the assets of the few largest companies account for a large proportion of the total. A survey carried out by the Monopolies Commission[1] showed that of the 908 manufacturing companies selected for study, 28 accounted for 50% of total assets. In 'drink' 5 firms accounted for 68% of assets, in 'tobacco' 1 firm for 71% and in 'chemicals' 4 firms for 79%. A very simple statistic (the 'concentration ratio' or proportion of assets or output accounted for by the three largest firms), has often been used to indicate the degree of concentration in an industry. Briefly, a few firms may be said to 'dominate' each main industry.

2. CONCENTRATION IS INCREASING

The evidence for this assertion is rather mixed.[2] Concentration ratios can be shown to have risen but their interpretation is difficult. The Monopolies Commission found, in the sample of companies already mentioned, that in 1961 the 28 largest companies had accounted for only 39% of assets. Further, there is now more evidence available about the extent of merger activity. Although the *number* of mergers in the U.K. decreased between 1965 and 1968, the average 'consideration' rose from £$\frac{1}{2}$ m. to nearly £3 m. Assets transferred as a result of mergers rose from 1$\frac{1}{2}$% of total company assets to 6$\frac{1}{2}$% between 1966 and 1968 (though this overstates the case as it ignores 'de-mergers', often due to bankruptcy). To 'explain' the merger process we shall first have to set out a rather fuller analysis of the firm than the skeleton often found in textbooks.

---

1 Monopolies Commission, H.C. 298, H.M.S.O., 1968–69.
2 R. Evely and I. Little, *Concentration in British Industry 1935–51*, Cambridge, 1960.

POLICY

3. COMPETITION AMONG THE GIANTS IS OLIGOPOLISTIC

Competition among very large firms is often 'oligopolistic' in nature. No firm feels able to inaugurate price competition without incurring retaliation from rivals so, instead, competition takes the form of advertising, exclusive trading networks, etc. Thus the manufacturers of electric lamps told the Monopolies Commission[1] that 'it was not possible . . . for one of them to raise prices without a disastrous loss of trade, nor was it possible for one of them to reduce prices without the others following'. The four largest groups accounted for 89% of the market and they tended, until very recently, to circulate identical lists of recommended prices. Whether an individual firm is an oligopolist or a monopolist is largely a matter of definition. U.K. anti-monopoly legislation has defined monopoly as the provision of over one-third of the market by one company. But although, since their merger, A.E.I. and Thorn-Electric between them accounted for 40% of the electric lamp market, the resulting market behaviour was oligopolistic in nature rather than monopolistic. At the other end of the scale there is, in most industries a long tail of smaller firms. They tend to follow the lead of giant firms but can often carve out special niches for themselves in special parts of the market either because they possess certain skills or because they are protected by geography and transport costs from distant competition. It is through the tail that the main pressures for competition come; existing medium-sized firms are potential rivals of existing giants and new entrants can seldom start off as large concerns. Existing giants show a very keen interest in erecting barriers to new competition.

These main features of industrial structure point to two possible areas of intervention. Firstly there is the possibility of intervening so as to alter the *structure* of industry. This is essentially the sort of rôle played by the I.R.C. Secondly one might interfere with the *price and output policies of* existing firms. This is essentially the rôle of the Monopolies Commission (and the National Board for Prices and Incomes). At the time of writing the overlapping functions of these two latter bodies are about to be merged.

---

1   Monopolies Commission, H.C. 4, H.M.S.O., 1968–9.

The Monopolies Commission and the Industrial Reorganisation Corporation

These two institutions illustrate in concrete form our schizophrenic approach to bigness. The Monopolies Commission was set up under the Monopolies and Mergers Act of 1948 (and 1965). From 1956, with the setting up of the Restrictive Trade Practices court, its field of operation was narrowed, but from 1965 not only has the Commission itself been enlarged but it also has been allowed a more powerful rôle in regard to mergers. The Industrial Reorganisation Corporation was set up in 1966. Its powers are fairly wide.[1]

'The Corporation may, for the purpose of promoting industrial efficiency and profitability and assisting the economy of the U.K. or any part of the U.K.:

(1) Promote or assist the reorganisation or development of any industry; or
(2) If requested to do so by the Secretary of State, establish or develop, or promote or assist the establishment or development of any industrial enterprise.'

It may draw on funds of up to £150 m. Most of its expenditure consists of granting of short term loans or the purchase of company shares. In its second year of operation it declared a small dividend.

The flavour of their investigations and the difference between their philosophies may be captured by a brief review of their activities in a single year, 1968–9. The Monopolies Commission produced in 1968 reports on clutch mechanisms, electric lamps, flat glass, men's haircuts and man-made cellulose fibres together with reports on the following merger proposals: Barclays Bank, Lloyds and Martins; Thorn Electrical and Radio Rentals; Thomson

1   *Industrial Reorganisation Corporation Report*, H.C. 286, H.M.S.O., 1968–9.

Newspapers and Crusha and Son; Rank and De la Rue. Their findings were:

that 'things done' by Automotive Products (clutch manufacturers) either operated or might be expected to operate against the public interest (though there was also a minority report);

that the electric lamp manufacturers acted against the public interest in publishing recommended prices;

that Pilkingtons did not operate against the public interest in spite of their 'monopoly' position in plate glass;

that there was no monopoly situation in men's hairdressing (!);

that Courtaulds operated against the public interest with regard to man-made cellulose fibres;

that the merger of Barclays, Lloyds and Martins would decrease competition in banking and therefore operate against the public interest;

that the merger of Thorn Electrical and Radio Rentals would not operate against the public interest;

that the merger of Crusha and Son with Thomson Newspapers would not be against the public interest;

that a merger of the Rank Organisation Ltd., and the De la Rue Co. Ltd., would not lead to any loss of competition but would be harmful to the efficiency of De la Rue.

Additionally the Commission produced a short general report on mergers. The hairdressing case may appear to sit rather oddly with the rest. The point, of course, is that a hairdresser may have a local monopoly.

Over the same period the I.R.C. had been *encouraging* mergers because 'the pace and scale of change do not yet match the needs of the national economy', because 'many of the production units in this country are small by comparison with most companies in international trade, whose operations are often based on a much larger market' and there is 'no evidence that we can rely on market forces alone to produce the necessary structural changes at the pace required'. Its report of March 1969 told of active intervention in the electronics industry to assist the merger between G.E.C. and

English Electric, in the scientific instruments industry to ensure that the U.S. firm of Kent (rather than Rank) obtained control of Cambridge Instruments, in ball bearings to bring the three leading firms together and in trawling to welcome a proposed merger between Associated Fisheries and the Ross Group (even though the Monopolies Commission had two years earlier declared against it). The ball bearings case was particularly interesting as the I.R.C. itself obtained control of one of the companies by a cash takeover of its controlling company thus giving itself a stronger hand in the negotiations.

The macroeconomic prices and incomes policy impinges directly on the prices and costs of individual firms both through its general statements and the N.B.P.I.'s investigations of particular situations. Our concern is with *prices* only. General policy on prices has gone through several stages since May 1965. Since the end of the first voluntary phase there has characteristically been a statement about the permitted general rate of increase[1] (presently three months, but twelve months immediately after devaluation) plus references to the Board. The criteria for its decisions have been a mixed bag but more and more emphasis has been given to questions of 'cost' and 'efficiency'. In the public sector the Board has undertaken a number of efficiency studies to ensure cost reductions and (possibly) also price reductions, and it is clearly anxious to apply these same techniques to the private sector. Thus, 'the traditional policy towards the problem of monopoly has been to try to restore competition. The fact has to be faced that this can rarely be done . . . the answer . . . is an efficiency study'.[2] The Board's yearning for a new-look anti-monopoly policy, coupled with one or two embarrassing occasions when the N.B.P.I. and the Monopolies Commission or Restrictive Trade Practices Court have been examining the same sector simultaneously, has been partly responsible for the merging of functions already referred to.

---

1 Since this was written, the prices and incomes policy has been virtually abandoned.
2 Natural Board for Incomes and Prices, 4th *Report*, H.M.S.O., July, 1968–July, 1969.

The traditional theory of the firm whose bare bones were presented in Chapter 2 is adequate for the discussion of simple monopoly. It shows how the monopolist is able to earn monopoly profit by restricting output and selling his goods at a price in excess of marginal cost (the excess depends on the elasticity of demand). But the more dynamic problems of expansion, growth and merger cannot be treated at all adequately within this framework. It is necessary to our discussion therefore to present a model of an individual firm's behaviour which, though simple, is able to say something about expansion and mergers. The main features of the theory (outlined in the appendix at the end of this chapter) are that:

(1) Expected earnings are 'discounted' to obtain their present value.

(2) The present value of expected earnings increases with planned expansion but at a decreasing rate, and may eventually fall.

(3) Profit maximisation is defined as maximising the net worth of the company or the present value of its earnings stream (π) *minus* the book value of its assets (K).

(4) Managers may or may not pursue a policy of profit maximisation.

(5) A group of outsiders may make a 'takeover bid' for a firm if its managers are not pursuing profit maximising policies.

Profit maximisation and expansion

In Chapter 3 emphasis was placed on 'stocks' as well as on 'flows'. This distinction is very important indeed in the analysis of company profits. Let the firm consider a 'horizon' of, say, twenty years. In each year it will expect (with varying degrees of uncertainty) a flow of profits, depending upon the state of the market, upon costs and upon planned assets. This series of flows can be reduced to a 'present value' or 'stock' by discounting it at the rate which is the interest paid to new holders of fixed-interest claims on the company (debenture holders and banks). Similarly the value of the company's present physical assets can be calculated. Let these present valuations be π and K respectively. Now the present net worth of the company is $(\pi - K)$ and I shall use profit maximisation to indicate maximising this quantity. Profits so calculated are net of the salaries of management and are either distributed to ordinary shareholders or retained in the company for reinvestment.

There are several fairly obvious reasons why the large corporation should take a long view about profit. Sometimes, however, it will take a very short view indeed (for example, in defending the present board against a takeover bid). The case for taking a long view can be described under the headings *goodwill* and *investment*. Both customers and employees have long memories; rapacious pricing or harsh wage policies may be long remembered. The amount that can be produced and sold in a given year is not therefore a function of price in that year alone but of policies in previous years as well. Behaviour of this type is sometimes (and wrongly) thought to be an exception to profit maximisation. It is, of course, merely an exception to crude short term maximisation. Similarly, current profits could be inflated by neglecting proper maintenance and by postponing new projects. Notice that if goodwill was unimportant in a particular market and if no long term investment was required it would be sensible to adopt short run profit maximisation on a continuing basis. The profit maximisation hypothesis, as we have interpreted it, is so general and so powerful that one is reluctant to abandon it!

We must now be a little more precise in defining the firm's problem. We envisage the managers of the firm as having to decide how much expansion to plan for during the planning period, that is to say up to the horizon. One accepts that there will be no absolute limits to the size of very large companies but this does not help very much with the actual planning decision: how much expansion should be undertaken now? The reason why there is (for practical purposes) no limit to size is that as soon as one force for expansion is spent, the managers are able to harness another. Thus decreasing costs will make expansion in one market profitable until the market is 'saturated', but diversification into other markets enables expansion to be sustained.

To say that there is practically no absolute limit to size is acceptable; but to say that large corporations can therefore plan and execute unlimited expansion is merely a confusion. There are several reasons for believing that the marginal costs of *rapid expansion* (rather than the costs of operating at a certain size) are high.

POLICY

1. FINANCIAL LIMITATIONS

Were the capital market perfect, the firm could simply borrow as much as it wanted at the going rate. In reality, the market is far from perfect and financial resources act as a real constraint on growth. For this reason most firms 'retain' a portion of profits. To make the principle clear, assume that a firm manages to retain the whole of its profits-after-tax. If the rate of profit-after-tax was 5% on assets then the assets of the company could grow *at most* by 5% if financed by internal sources. Had half of the profit been retained, the maximum growth rate permitted by internally provided finance would have been $2\frac{1}{2}\%$. More loosely, the amount of money a firm will be able to get hold of is likely to depend on the rates of profit it has recently experienced or is expected to experience. It is common to talk of this as a constraint, pure and simple. Alternatively, and more realistically, it makes the *marginal cost of finance* very high beyond a certain point. That is, the firm has to use resources in searching for extra finance which it will then have to service on relatively unfavourable terms.

2. MANAGERIAL LIMITATIONS

Though managers can be hired just like other inputs, there is a limit on the rate at which the inner management structure of the firm (its 'core') is able to absorb new managers and markets. Mrs. Penrose[1] argued convincingly over a decade ago that this provides a real constraint on the *rate of growth* of large corporations. Again it seems preferable to bring this in as a factor pushing up the marginal costs of growth. There is no reason why the firm should not press ahead with ill-considered expansion; it is merely that the price of this will perhaps be poor marketing, inferior organisation and so on.

These two limitations on growth, financial and managerial, imply that in spite of economies of scale and diversification the present value of expected profits (π) will, at best, increase at a decreasing rate (as shown in the appendix to this chapter) as more expansion is

---

1   E. Penrose, *The Theory of the Growth of the Firm*, London, 1959.

planned. If this is so, there will be an optimum amount of expansion, i.e., one that maximises $(\pi - K)$. If the corporation goes to the capital market for its extra finance the market price per share will itself be maximised at this same optimum level.

However, there are reasons for believing that most corporations do not, in fact, pursue profit maximisation. At bottom this is due to the well-known 'divorce' of ownership from control; the ordinary shares are owned by a large number of institutions and individuals who rarely (certainly not at the usual annual meeting) have the opportunity to organise themselves into a coherent group, while the inner core of top management (with some places on the board) retains effective control over company policy. It has been pointed out (particularly by Galbraith) that the managers of a company are able to exercise a lot of control over their environment in other ways—by skilful use of advertising campaigns, by a controlled programme of technical research and by long term agreements with principal unions.

Several alternatives to profit maximisation are open. Among those commonly suggested in the literature, growth or sales maximisation (subject to some minimum profits constraint) has been prominent. Managers would certainly be behaving rationally if they pursued the goal of size, for the evidence is that salaries are related to sales or assets which, it is assumed, bear some relation to the 'responsibilities' of the job. But they dare not let share prices fall below a certain minimum as this will make it difficult to raise new finance at a later stage. The way in which managers behave in this type of situation can be described either in terms of *optimising* or in terms of *satisficing*. On the first approach managers seek to maximise the present value of their expected lifetime incomes. To achieve this they will tend to pursue a 'mix' of growth and profits maximisation for their present company, thus keeping the profits record respectable at the same time as gaining status in the eyes of other managers. On the second approach, managers recognise the uncertain nature of business life and simply aim at achieving a number of minimum goals, for example, to earn a gross return on asssts of 15%, to expand sales by not less than 5%, to keep share prices above £120 each, to keep the share of the market to not less than 30%, and so on. These are merely rules of thumb for avoiding disaster; there is no conscious attempt to maximise anything. This latter *behavioural* approach is defective (in my view)[1] in that it provides no rule of thumb for choosing among the rules of thumb. If some rules are discarded as 'bad' or others adopted as 'good', there must be some criterion for choosing between them. The obvious criterion is the present value of managerial income. Whether an individual manager puts more stress on profits or on growth then depends largely on his method of salary payment—the larger the 'bonus' element (depending on profits) or the larger his stake in the company's equity the greater weight is he likely to attach to profits.

The conclusion to be drawn is as follows: under profit maximisation the managers will choose that bundle of assets, markets and prices that maximises the net present worth of the company; but within certain broad limits, managers can exercise discretion as to how far they wish to pursue profits or some other objective.

Takeovers and mergers

The market (in this case the stock market) provides in principle a very neat check on managerial discretion—the takeover bid. If a group of outsiders comes to believe that, under different management, it would be possible to increase the net present worth of the company and therefore permit higher share prices, it will be in their interests to make an 'offer' for sufficient ordinary shares as will gain them effective control over policy. (Thus, in the appendix, it will pay them to offer up to $(1 + a)$ per share.) In this light the takeover bid is an effective substitute for shareholder control and *forces* firms to pursue the goal of profit maximisation. Unfortunately the takeover market is a highly imperfect one, mainly because the participants tend to be ill-informed. It is typically in the interests of the existing board to claim that the share price *understates* the present net worth of the company because new, efficient policies

---

1   cf. R. M. Cyert and J. C. March, *A Behavioural Theory of the Firm*, New Jersey, 1963.

are in hand whose results have, to date, not been apparent. It is in the interests of the bidder to claim that the present price is, if anything, an over-valuation if present policies continue, and to point to defects in the presentation of previous results (even to alleged fraud). The ordinary shareholder has little in the way of solid evidence on which to base his judgement. In the U.K. the City Takeover Panel has exercised some modest improvement by drawing up a (voluntary) code of conduct.

Conventionally, the 'outsider' is another company in the same broad field of operation, seeking the advantages of '*vertical*' or '*horizontal*' integration; these are well-known. Vertical integration is the bringing together of the successive stages of an industrial process (e.g., the old G.K.N. combination of steel production and bolt and nail making), its chief disadvantage being that managers at the end of the chain no longer search for the cheapest sources of supply. Horizontal integration is the bringing together of various units at a given stage (e.g., the amalgamation of chains of retail shops or of motor manufacturers), its chief disadvantage being the potential increase in market power. Both these sets of disadvantages may or may not be outweighed by increases in efficiency. At any rate the things to look for are fairly straightforward. But a third type of merger (the *conglomerate*) is of increasing importance, perhaps 40% of the total. A conglomerate operates in a number of apparently unrelated fields (e.g., Unilever); the old checks of dis-economies of scale and market saturation do not operate. Its managers, as we have already noticed, will be under pressure to 'grow', to 'diversify'. The central 'core' of managers is not specialised in one field; it consists in generalised managerial talent which (though hiring production engineers and plant managers) organises, markets products and sets research in train. It is as though the optimum structure of industry is such that will best use the existing stock of generalised managerial talent. Growth and acquisition are simply devices for bringing about an optimum structure. As already noticed there are two reasons for doubting the efficiency of this process, (1) firms are able effectively to raise protective barriers between inner management and usual market forces and (2) shareholders and others are badly informed. A deficiency of knowledge on the part of shareholders led the Monopolies Commission to make the following observation,

> 'It is said that if the shareholders of the firm being bid for accepted the offer, then by implication, they took the view that the bidding firm would use the assets of the firm more efficiently and their judgement on this point should be regarded by the Commission as conclusive. We reject this argument . . . the connection between the shareholders' assessment of a takeover offer and their assessment of the effects of the takeover on efficiency is not as direct or as straightforward as the argument suggests, and may be tenuous, remote or even non-existent, according to the particular circumstances.'[1]

The criterion they suggest (though immensely difficult to use in practice) is whether or not the proposed merger or takeover improves the allocation of resources.

Conclusion

The main policy objectives are:

(1) An optimum industrial structure
(2) Efficient production methods
(3) Consumer protection.

The organs of policy discussed in this chapter have necessarily been 'interventionist'—the Monopolies Commission, the I.R.C., the N.B.P.I. The theoretical rationale for this selective or even discriminatory approach is that no easy general rules exist for solving the three types of problem just mentioned. Interference can be general only as long as problems are general. But bigness gives rise to unique problems sector by sector; the legislator or functionary who seeks to improve must first analyse. Whether an industry is publicly or privately owned the problems, and hence the policy tools required to deal with them, are much the same. Bigness calls for interventionism and eclecticism.

---

1 Monopolies Commission, H.C. 298, H.M.S.O., 1968–9.

Appendix

A THEORY OF THE FIRM

Underlying the discussion of profits, growth and market valuation has been a simple model of the following type:

π = present value of expected after-tax profits, discounted at a rate i over T years

K = value of current assets

$V = \pi - K$ = net present worth.

If net present worth is zero the firm is 'worth' only what can be raised by disposing of its assets (K). What is the best value of K? That is to say, how much current expansion should there be? Assume that π increases as K increases, but at a decreasing rate as illustrated in the figure:

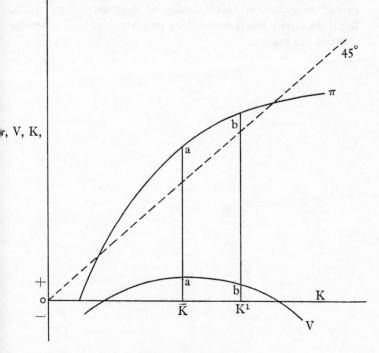

Fig. 9. A Firm's Net Present Worth

There is no absolute barrier to growth, i.e., π increases; it is simply that growth becomes unprofitable beyond a certain point. The point of maximum net worth (a) is when assets are at $\overline{K}$. *If* expansion is to be financed by the issue of ordinary shares and *if* the market is well-informed and *if* managers are profit maximisers, the market valuation of shares will stand at $(1 + a)$ of their nominal value.

Suppose for a moment that managers' 'tastes' are such that they prefer greater expansion to the point K^1. On the assumptions we have made, share prices will stand at only $(1 + b)$. It would then pay a group of outsiders to offer up to $(1 + a)$ per share in order to obtain control of the company. Outsiders would normally argue during such a takeover bid that the whole π curve could be moved upward under different management. If the takeover mechanism was working properly, firms would be forced to carry out that amount of expansion which maximised their net present worth. But if the mechanism is not working properly there is no guarantee that this will happen.

15 THE SOCIAL SERVICES

Taxes and benefits

Expenditure on the social services by U.K. public authorities, both local and central, grew roughly twice as rapidly during the 1960s as did the gross national product (G.N.P.). By 1969, including transfer payments, it amounted to about one quarter of the G.N.P. There are several reasons for expecting that this trend will continue: the proportion of non-working to working population will continue to rise; technical advances in medicine (transplant surgery is the most dramatic but there are dozens of more humdrum ones) are likely to accelerate; people will demand higher standards in the existing services (for example, the comfort of outpatient departments). One may add the 'value judgement' that more money income *ought* to be transferred to the poorer members of the community.

For practical and for analytical reasons it will be useful to distinguish between decisions about the use of real resources (labour, cement, steel) and the mere transfer of money. Roughly speaking (because money grants to individuals are involved in some of them), those items involving the use of real resources are education, the national health service, local welfare services, child care, school meals and milk, welfare foods and housing. But social security benefits—national insurance and industrial injuries, war pensions, retirement pensions, supplementary benefits and family allowances—are simply transfers of spending power between individuals. Taking the country as a whole, payments of this sort cancel each other out and do not, therefore, appear in the national income accounts.

Consider ordinary consumer goods as against school building. Real resources, for instance those used in building shops, could be diverted to schools depending on the *amount* of taxation raised. Taxation in this context is merely a device for giving the state enough money to effect the transfer of real resources that it wishes. If the state owned all the resources it could, of course, effect the transfer directly; but it would still need to use a tax weapon of some type to prevent inflationary pressure in the consumer goods sector.

In real terms the amount of resources that needs diverting in order to produce a given amount of school building depends on technical conditions. The money equivalent is the amount of extra taxation needed to cover the cost of the programme. Again, economic growth implies a potential improvement so that it might be possible to have more consumer goods *and* more schools. The 'buoyancy' of tax revenue as incomes increase ensures that some transfer of real resources can be achieved relatively painlessly even in a capitalist system. (Indeed the replacement of fixed money taxes with income related taxes was a major factor in the rise of the modern state.) The slower the rate of economic growth the more painful will the choice become between schools and consumer goods.

Money transfers, at a first approximation, are simply a way of redistributing the total of consumer goods between persons. The amount of redistribution achieved depends not on the amount of taxation but on its *progressiveness*. (A progressive tax system is one under which those with higher incomes pay a larger proportion in tax.)

Taxation, therefore, features centrally in both the reallocation and the redistribution questions. It is the main instrument of policy. The three main types of U.K. tax are those on income (progressive and bringing in over 40% of revenue), those on expenditure (mildly regressive and bringing in nearly 40% of revenue) and national insurance contributions (very regressive and bringing in over 15% of revenue). The overall effect of the tax structure is, perhaps surprisingly, more or less neutral with very slight traces of progression in recent years.

Redistributive effect of benefits

It is possible, in a rough and ready sort of way, to work out the redistributive effects of social benefits (both in cash and in kind) and to compare these with the effects of the tax structure itself. Cash payments are relatively easy to establish given the size and age composition of the family, but benefits in kind can be apportioned to households only in rather an arbitrary fashion. While some cannot be allocated to individuals at all (police, defence, administration), others like health and education, can reasonably be said to provide direct or indirect benefits on a proportionate basis. (Notice that the term 'benefit' is used here in rather a loose way, meaning a transfer in cash or kind; this should not be confused with its more specialised use in Chapter 7.) Apart from the conceptual and statistical difficulties of this procedure, there is the objection that middle-class families are able to manipulate the state-provided education and health services to their own advantage. If this were so, calculations on the present basis would overstate the amount of redistribution in kind.

Figure 10 summarises the position for a family of two adults and three children[1] based on a family expenditure survey of 1967.

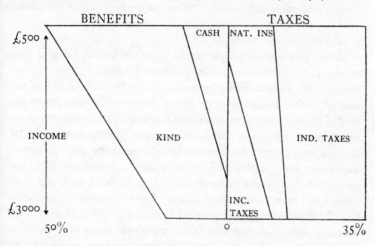

Fig. 10. Per cent of Original Income Plus Cash Benefits

The right hand side of the figure shows the overall pattern of the tax structure itself to be about neutral. But benefits in cash and in kind were progressive; altogether, families with an original income of over about £1500 (per annum) were made' worse off' as a result of

1   See *Economic Trends*, no. 184, Feb. 1969, pp. xi–xxxix.

the whole welfare package, and those with an original income of under £1200 were made 'better off'. It is also the case, though not shown in the figure, that the welfare package is progressive with respect to size of family. Clearly then the state provision of benefits has an important effect on the redistribution of real income. These must not be forgotten in discussions of the various ways of financing the provision of benefits in kind.

Financing benefits in kind

The rising importance of social service expenditure, together with the apparent unpopularity of high marginal rates of taxation, has led to a search for different methods of finance, principally in health, education and housing. Three methods require discussion.

1. FEES PLUS MEANS TESTS

Under this system people would pay fees for the benefits they receive but exemption or rebate could be obtained by those on low incomes. At present, fees play a minor role. Only about 4% of the cost of welfare foods is met by direct charges and about 5% of the cost of general medical services. But in some areas of policy, fees are rather more important. Examples are prescription charges, dental charges and charges for home-helps. Means tests are, of course, unpopular for excellent historical reasons. Moreover they are inefficient. People are rather badly informed about their rights to rebates and exemptions; applicants can face a whole battery of means tests from different departments of the same public authority. The marginal cost of making sure that extra people know their rights is high and must include large items of expenditure on publicity (the school meals case is particularly easy because the schools have ready-made channels of communication with parents). (One of the attractions, by the way, of a 'negative' income tax is the ease with which it would apparently solve the means test problem.) Another argument against the fees solution is that, even allowing for means tests, its redistributive effect would be clearly regressive. Finally the decision to make use of a service would depend on income as well as on 'need'. Many have argued that this would be a good thing, that it would discourage 'malingering'. But it would be repugnant if the decision as to whether to consult (say) a doctor about a child's illness had to depend upon income.

2. CONTRIBUTIONS

In the U.K. the provision of a major social benefit in cash (pensions) is increasingly to be financed out of contributions rather than taxes. Given that a total mount of service is to be provided, one's judgement must hinge upon the possibility of regressiveness. Present national insurance and health contributions are clearly regressive (see Fig. 10). But if contributions were proportional to income (together with an employer's contribution) the redistributive effects would be more complicated. Take two extreme positions. If the alternative means of finance was income tax and if employers managed to 'pass on' their own contributions to consumers the overall effect would be definitely regressive. But if the alternative was indirect taxation and employers managed to pass on a very little of their own contributions the effect would probably be slightly progressive. A difficulty is to locate the real incidence of the contribution as distinct from its initial impact. A complication here is that people seem to feel they have 'earned' a benefit if they have paid contributions as against taxes.

3. MARKETS PLUS VOUCHERS

At the most trivial level the argument for putting a greater reliance on the free market in, say, health and education is financial; that the state cannot 'afford' to expand these services while the private sector can. The argument is not really economic at all but political. The economic problem is the availability of real resources, the political is how much in the way of real resources should be diverted (through tax policies) to the public sector. Less trivially, the advantages of the market are said to be:

> greater individual choice,
> greater incentives for efficiency,
> elimination of shortages.

Against these must be set the usual drawbacks of markets—the

149

difficulties that individuals experience in making a well-informed choice, the possible abuse of local monopoly power and the generation of externalities.[1] They are much more worrying in the social services than in, say, the baked beans market. But the biggest potential disadvantage is that the poor would suffer. Some device would therefore be needed to prevent this (just as a means test device would be needed if charges were widely introduced). One such device would be the issuing of 'vouchers' which would safeguard the interests of the poor and at the same time enable the advantages of the market to be retained. Each family would be given a voucher for education, health or housing which it could supplement if it wished.

As in our general discussion of markets in Chapter 4, there are basically two sets of objections to the 'markets plus vouchers' solution:

(1) Technical difficulties (externalities, pricing policies, etc.),
(2) Moral objections concerned with paternalism, equality and social cohesion.

Even a generous voucher scheme would make only a small dent in the set of objections under (2) and non-earmarked vouchers would be open to abuse, people who value education only a little swapping them for other goods. Such exercise of choice is a doubtful advantage.

Taxes and efficiency

The reason for looking at these various alternative means of financing the social services was the unpopularity of increases in income tax. Behind this unpopularity is the feeling that income tax is 'disincentive', in other words, it has harmful effects on efficiency and saving and eventually on the volume of real resources available.

A priori an increase in income tax rates may affect in either way willingness of individuals to work. As 'leisure' becomes less expensive (in relation to other 'goods'), the substitution effect suggests that

---

1 For a more detailed critical account see my 'The New Right: A Critique', *Fabian Tract* (387) 1968.

individuals will choose to spend less time each day at work and more time 'consuming' leisure. But the income effect[1] suggests that as real income falls (following the tax increase) individuals *may* wish to offer more labour. This latter result would be particularly plausible if he was trying to maximise retirement income. Empirical work in this field is notoriously difficult to interpret as answers to question-naires are unreliable (as predictors of behaviour) and as knowledge of effective tax rates is extremely sketchy. Many overestimate this as a result of ignoring earned income allowance; two-ninths earned income allowance reduces the U.K. standard rate of income tax to about 30%. Many believe, however, that they pay at the nominal standard rate.[2] Statistical work is difficult to interpret because other important variables dominate taxation in the overall explana-tion of working hours (union arrangements, non-monetary incentives, legislation, etc.). Additionally, the method of international com-parisons is very misleading unless the income equivalents are correctly calculated and the whole 'welfare package' examined. Lastly, the existence of pressure groups is not evidence of disincen-tive, merely of unpopularity.

If income tax really is disincentive there will be a certain amount of 'trade-off' between equality and prosperity. A major gap in our knowledge of the economic system is the shape of this trade-off. Over the range relevant to discussion in the U.K. (plus or minus five new pence in the pound), there are two reasons for believing that the trade-off will not be significant in real terms, though it may be politically.

(1) There are several weak links in the causal chain. Hours worked are only weakly related to tax rates, effort expanded to hours worked and work done to effort expended.

(2) It is probable that a high proportion of total economic

---

1   See page 18 for an explanation of income and substitution effects. It may be that the supply curve for labour services is backward sloping over certain ranges.
2   C. V. Brown and D. A. Dawson, *Personal Taxation, Incentive and Tax Reform*, P.E.P. Broadsheet 506, Jan. 1969.

POLICY

growth can be accounted for by technological progress.[1]
There is no plausible link between *income* tax rates and the
rate of growth of technical knowledge.

The poor

In spite of rising affluence there are still several million people in
the U.K. (and many more in the U.S.A.) who can fairly be described
as living in poverty. Depending on how poverty is defined (usually
in terms of social security scales of benefit)[2] the U.K. figure can be
placed in the range four to seven million. What should be done about
the poor? The proximate causes of poverty are widely known—
low pay, large families, sickness, disablement, widowhood, old age,
unemployment. The present system consists of a bundle of grants
and allowances topped up, where necessary, by social security
payments. It will be convenient to refer to this as the 'poverty
bundle'. The most obvious way of eliminating poverty would be to
raise the various cash benefits, though even this would do little for
those employed but on low pay.

The main arguments against increasing the poverty bundle
concern the 'burden' of taxation and the disincentive effects of
generous social security payments. Unfortunately, with the traditional income tax system, it is not possible to do anything for the
really poor. A reduction in the lowest rates of tax will not benefit
those too poor to pay and at all; neither will an increase in tax-
allowances (indeed an increase is more helpful to the better off).

---

1   F. F. Denison, *The Sources of Economic Growth in the U.S. and the
Alternatives before us*, New York, 1962.
2   Poverty is most frequently defined in terms of social security scales.
Thus a family earning less than, say, 140% of its social security entitlement
could be described as living in poverty. This means, of course, that poverty
is being explained in a relative, not an absolute, fashion and that there will
be a jump in the number of families defined as living in poverty whenever
the scale of social security payments increases. But it would be absurd to
insist on an absolute definition. That poverty is defined in this way does, of
course, mean that western countries will continue to feel that they have a
poverty problem even though the masses in poor countries may be desperately
poor.

152

THE SOCIAL SERVICES

A comparison of the three main possibilities may be made with reference to Figure 11 (overleaf).

I. POVERTY BUNDLE PLUS INCOME TAX

The figure represents a much simplified form of U.K. tax system for a given family. Below a critical level the family can have its income made up to (S), the social security floor, by means of the poverty bundle. But there will be some families (whose heads of household are in full time employment) receiving incomes below (S). At some level of income higher than (S) the family would pay tax at a standard marginal rate. The figure ignores, therefore, the very low and the very high marginal tax rates. Clearly neither a change in the slope of the line $\alpha\beta$ nor an upward shift would be of any direct help to the poor.

2. NEGATIVE INCOME TAX

It would be possible, in principle, to scrap the whole of the poverty bundle and, instead, to devise a simple income tax structure incorporating both positive and 'negative' taxes. Each family would complete a questionnaire about its financial means and its own internal structure (size, ages, etc.) just as under the income tax system. An advantage claimed for such a system is that some cash benefits (family allowances, state pensions) are given regardless of 'need'. A relatively painless test would ensure that only those 'in need' received the benefits. The figure shows a flat rate negative tax designed to ensure a post-tax income at least as great as the social security floor. A family with no income would receive a subsidy equal to $(-T)$. Unlike the present system, the amount of subsidy would *not* depend on whether the wage-earner was in employment.

A disadvantage of the proposal is that emergencies like ill-health, unemployment and widowhood often arise with little warning and require immediate action; the organisation responsible for making cash payments to individuals should be geared to, say, a weekly cycle of operations. But tax revenue authorities are used to operating on an annual cycle. So advocates of the negative income tax are usually also advocates of technical and administrative change in the

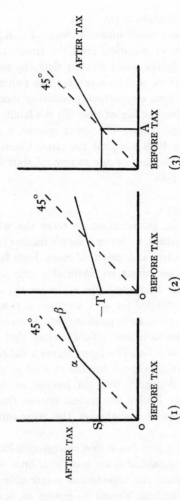

Fig. 11. Alternative Tax Systems

whole organisational structure. Much current controversy centres around the realism of expecting such change in the near future. Notice too that a really efficient negative income tax would produce as a by-product a readily useable 'means test' for benefits in kind.

3. CASH GRANTS PLUS INCOME TAX

Under this system each family would be paid a cash allowance (payable like present family allowances) at least equal to the appropriate current social security level. This would imply a cash grant of (A). Present cash payments would, of course, be scrapped. Revenue would be obtained by taxing all incomes other than the cash grant at, say, a single flat rate (probably of the order of 30–35 %). An advantage of such a scheme would be that the whole apparatus of income tax codes would no longer be necessary. On the other hand the Ministry of Social Security would have to set up new and complex machinery to calculate cash entitlements and, perhaps, actually handle payments. Like the negative income tax it would help all the poor whether they happened to be in employment or not. But unlike the negative income tax it could be flexible in emergency situations. (An interesting sociological effect would be the decreasing importance of the wage earner in total family income.)

On a straight comparison between methods (1), (2) and (3), the latter two are each preferable to the first so far as the employed person on low pay is concerned. Is there a simple way of modifying (1) so as to remove this very great disadvantage? Two sorts of modification are possible; one could allow the social security floor to operate for everyone regardless of whether or not he is unemployed (a minimum income) or one could introduce minimum wage legislation.

Roughly speaking the minimum income is 'liberal' and the minimum wage 'interventionist'. The argument against the minimum income is that it is disincentive. No wage-earner getting less than the minimum would have anything to gain by working more. (Neither, on the face of it, is there any incentive to remain in employment under the present system; but this is minimised by the use of the 'wage-stop'.) The present system could be converted into a minimum income system by improvements in the poverty bundle *plus* removal of the wage stop *plus* payment of social security benefits to those in employment.

Only two points need to be made here about minimum wage legislation. The expected effects depend upon the basic model used, a competitive model suggesting an increase in unemployment the extent of which depends on the elasticity of demand and supply of labour *in the low wage sector*. At the other extreme, if the wage rate were merely a matter of power or bargaining strength there would simply be, as a result of minimum wage legislation, a direct re-distribution of income with no unemployment effects. Unfortunately, bargaining power is weak in the low wage sector so it would be unreasonable not to expect actual or disguised unemployment. By disguised unemployment we mean, for example, part-time workers who, having failed to find work at the new rates, withdraw from the labour market altogether. It would therefore be necessary to combine minimum wage legislation with generous unemployment benefit, redundancy pay and industrial retraining (see Chapter 18).

Political choice

The structure of the welfare state is determined by political (non-market) decision-making processes. It will be useful, therefore, to consider these in the remaining parts of this chapter. A great difficulty is that they are very complex and any simple model is bound to be misleading. However, it is possible to make the following simple generalisation in the case of goods that are publicly provided at a zero price for 'consumption' by individuals:

(1) There will be shortages of these goods with the usual symptoms of excess demand, queues, waiting lists, etc. Consequently there will be complaints by individuals that supply should be increased.

(2) Nevertheless it is impossible to say, in general, whether public provision would exceed or fall short of some alternative method of provision through the market.

To illustrate in terms of the national health service, there will be waiting lists for operations, shortages of beds and so on, but nevertheless we cannot know whether more or less medical care would result under free market conditions.

To establish the second of these two propositions we shall need the concept of the *tax-price*. In deciding whether to support a proposed expansion in the social services the voter will take into account the probable effects on the amount of taxation he will consequently have to pay.[1] The tax-price is the tax cost to him of increasing state provision by one unit. What determines this tax-price? Two factors are relevant (apart from tax evasion); the tax structure and the individual's place in the hierarchy of incomes. Given these two pieces of information and the cost of providing the good, it will be possible to calculate the individual's tax-price. Unlike market prices, they will, of course, differ from one individual to another.

Consider the outcome in terms of two classes, the 'rich' and the 'poor'. If the poor pay little or no tax (they have low or even zero tax-prices) and they have a strong liking for the good, and if also the rich behave to some degree altruistically, it is likely that people will vote for a large quantity to be provided. Conversely, if tax-prices facing the poor are high, they have no strong liking for the good and the rich behave selfishly, people are likely to vote for only a small quantity of the good. Thus the two forces working for a high level of public provision that cannot make themselves felt in a free market are altruism (on the part of the better off) and a strong desire for the good (for instance, education) among the worse off. The main force working against a high level of public provision is the high tax-price faced by the better off.

As people do not vote separately on issues such as education but have to accept or reject whole bundles of policies, there will be only a weak link between the whole tax-price-taste structure and the political outcome. But there is one simple circumstance in which the outcome is quite clear, that of single-issue simple majority voting.

---

1   In the jargon of Part I, the voter will have a marginal demand price that varies with income. Whenever his tax-price exceeds his marginal demand price he will vote for social service expenditure to be curtailed.

POLICY

Assume that each voter has a 'most preferred' outcome (referred to in the literature as the single-peakedness assumption) and that these outcomes can be set out along a linear scale as below.[1] The median outcome is, in this case, that preferred by individual (2). Further, the median outcome will *always* emerge under a system of simple majority rule. Any proposal to move from a non-median outcome

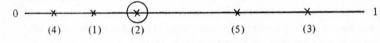

Most preferred outcomes

to the median will command a simple majority, while any proposal to move from the latter will be defeated. For example, a proposal to move from (5) to (2) will be opposed by individuals (3) and (5) but supported by the other three. Similarly a proposal to move from (2) to (1) will be supported by (4) and (1) but opposed by individuals (2), (5) and (3). If the further assumption is made that the preferences of that voter who turns out to be median is 'representative', the total provided publicly will be greater than the (alternative) private provision whenever the median voter's tax-price is less than the (alternative) market price. However, as the assumptions required to reach this particular result are rather stringent, it will be more useful to maintain a general agnosticism as to whether private or public provision would be the greater.

Now suppose, the amount of public provision having been determined, that the goods or services (say hospital places) are made available at zero prices. The first of our two propositions will then hold with waiting lists, for instance, as symptoms of excess demand. But these symptoms merely imply that a below market clearing price has been adopted; and this may be highly desirable on re-distributive grounds. They imply nothing at all (as some advocates of free markets have seemed to believe) about whether there is under- or over-provision of the good itself. Queues and shortages

---

1   See H. Hotelling, 'Stability in Competition', *Economic Journal* (39), 1929.

do not, in themselves, prove that more would be provided through the market.

A more general, if obvious, point can be made about democracy and the welfare state. Both services in cash and in kind require that at least some voters will receive fewer consumer goods than before. Given the 'tastes' of individuals (including their levels of ignorance and selfishness), it will be possible to receive majority support up to a certain size of programme. Now the imperfections of the political choice process are (perhaps fortunately) such that a government is able, particularly for short periods of time, to depart sub-substantially from the policy that would command the support of most voters. There is no reason, of course, why one should accept a majority view or any other view as 'right', but it is important to a scientific study of politico-economic processes that social scientists should continue their attempts to compare market and non-market decision-making processes with one another.

Summary

Taxes are the main policy instrument of the welfare state enabling resources to be diverted to the public sector and consumer goods to be redistributed among persons. The tax structure is approximately 'neutral' over a wide range of incomes but the whole tax-benefit structure is 'progressive' due to the progressive nature of all benefits. Charges, contributions and markets all have disadvantages as alternative methods of financing further expansion of the welfare state but the case that extra income tax finance would act as a disincentive is doubtful. The present system does too little to help the really poor and there are interesting alternatives[1] including negative income tax, minimum wage legislation and modifications in the 'poverty bundle'.

---

1 Since this chapter was written the Family Income Supplement (FIS) has been introduced. Essentially it is a partial form of negative income tax. Applicants may claim an allowance equal to 50% of the difference between their earnings and their hypothetical social security entitlements. Thus direct relief can be given to those in work. However, the total amount of public money involved is small as the need for specific claims to be made has led to a disappointing take up rate in spite of extensive publicity.

16 HOUSING POLICY

Housing needs

The housing situation in the U.K. illustrates some of the main themes of this book. There is an extensive free market in housing in which rents, house prices and new construction are determined by the 'laws of supply and demand' and enough information about this market to be able to make some intelligent guesses about demand elasticities. But there is also a major part of the market in which rents are either controlled by law or fixed by local authorities. Apart from these controls governments have a variety of instruments at their disposal for affecting the housing situation. They will, of course, be concerned with questions of welfare as much as efficiency. Some people will be too poor to provide themselves with adequate housing, others too feckless. Governments will also have to keep in mind the wider issues of urban planning and the environment.

A basic feature is that the *stock* of housing is very large in relation to the annual flow of new housing. The stock is of the order of eighteen million[1] dwellings and the flow of the order of 350,000 to 400,000, i.e., about 2% is added to the stock each year. This means that the housing situation is dominated by the stock inherited from the past; it is rather insensitive to quite large changes in the current house-building programme. Historically, the first objective of housing policy since the Second World War has been to increase the rate of building. Hence the targets of 300,000 per year (in the early 1950s) and of 500,000 per year (in the mid-1960s). More recently policy has shifted away from targets to concern with the quality of the stock and the rate of deterioration of old houses.[2] The average age of the U.K. housing stock is about fifty-five years and there are a great many, perhaps 1·8 million, that are 'unfit' (10% of the stock).

A conventional and very useful way of forecasting housing needs is as follows. One obtains projections of future population by age

---

1   *Housing Statistics*, no. 19, H.M.S.O., Nov. 1970.
2   *Old Houses into New Homes*, Cmnd. 3602, H.M.S.O., 1968.

and sex. These are sensitive to birth rates so a number of estimates is usually made. Given the size and composition of the population it is possible to make reasonable guesses at the number of future households by applying 'headship rates'. The headship rate of adult males of working age will be very high indeed and that of young single females of working age, rather low. The number of households thus obtained is a measure of the 'need' for housing. Notice that need is here defined independently of money demand. Whether or not people can afford to house themselves is a different question. However, once need has been measured it is, in principle, a fairly simple matter to calculate the amount of new construction required. The figures are conjectural but they are of the order of magnitude appropriate to U.K. needs over the next decade or so.[1]

Stock of housing at		Households at beginning	
beginning of planning			
period	18·0m	of planning period	18·0m
—Losses due to demolition,			
slum clearance, etc,	1·5m	+New households formed	
+New housing to be built	3·0m	during period	1·5m
	———	Stock required at end of	———
Stock at end of period	19·5m	period	19·5m

The figure under 'losses' is fairly arbitrary: the bigger the rate of demolition and renewal the higher it will be. The annual construction programme is sensitive to the demolition rate. If it were only 0·5 m over the period the annual construction required would fall to about 200,000. If it were as much as 2·5 m it would rise to 400,000.

Popular discussion has centred around the question of whether or not the housing *shortage* has disappeared. In the crude sense that households will soon be at least equal in number to dwelling units it is correct to talk of an overall balance. But it would be wrong, for various reasons, to conclude that the 'shortage' is over.

---

1   See P. A. Stone, *Urban Development in Britain: Standards, Costs and Resources 1964–2004*, vol. 1, N.I.E.S.R., 1970.; and H. W. Richardson and J. Vipond, 'Housing in the 1970s', *Lloyds' Bank Review*, April 1970.

The regional balance is uneven, so that acute shortages persist in Greater London along with surpluses in East Anglia and Wales. Even if this balance were redressed, there would remain the challenge of bringing sub-standard housing up to the current average or of replacing it altogether. Whether the housing *problem* has disappeared is not a question of objective scientific fact but depends upon one's priorities for policy, i.e., it is a normative question.

A simple model of the housing market

The following model gives a stylised account of the main features of the U.K. housing market. This is not a single market but an inter-related set of local ones; the very richness of the housing situation defies a simple supply and demand approach. A fundamental difficulty is the lack of a single homogeneous commodity, 'housing'. Houses will differ in all sorts of ways, in size, in state of repair, in surroundings, in amenities like gardens and garages and in style. There are almost as many commodities as there are separate houses. Nevertheless it will be assumed for the sake of the present discussion that some sort of standard measure can be concocted.

Only three sectors will be considered—local authority rented houses, private tenancies and houses for owner occupation.

1. Let H be the total stock of council houses, allocated on a waiting list basis. For simplicity it is assumed that people wanting council houses will have to go to the private rented sector if a council house is not allocated to them.
2. Let the demand for private tenancies be

$$D_r = D_r(r,P,Y) - H \qquad \text{(demand function)}$$

where,

r is weekly rent,
P is the price of owner-occupied housing,
Y is average household income.

Let the supply of private tenancies be

$$S_r = S_r(r), \qquad \text{(supply function)}$$

where a low price elasticity of supply is assumed.

If price is determined competitively we have

$$D_r = S_r \qquad \text{(equilibrium condition)}.$$

The case where rent is not determined competitively will have to be discussed in a moment.

3. Let the demand for houses for owner-occupation be

$$D_o = D_o(r,P,Y,A,F) \qquad \text{(demand function)}$$

where A is a variable representing household assets,
and F is a variable representing the degree of financial stringency. Supply is given by

$$S_o = S_o(P). \qquad \text{(supply function)}$$

Finally,

$$D_o = S_o. \qquad \text{(equilibrium condition)}$$

The elasticity of supply will be low in the short term but may be quite high in the longer term depending on the productivity of the construction industries and the supply of land.

It is instructive to consider what may happen as each of the independent variables is altered. These are H, Y, A, and F.

ALTERATIONS IN H

If local authorities decide to produce more council houses pressure on the private rented market will ease. r will tend to fall relative to prices in general. In fact, only tenants who are on the margin of moving will notice that r is falling as new contracts come to be negotiated. Sitting tenants will continue to pay at the old rates. The fall in rents will in turn bring about some substitution from owner-occupation demand to tenancy demand; the fall in rents will be moderated and there will be some fall in the price of owner-occupied houses.

ALTERATIONS IN Y

As average incomes rise, the demand for most types of housing will rise. Income elasticities of demand will not be uniform over housing of different quality. Very poor housing may be an inferior good (that is, it may have a negative income elasticity) while new housing for owner-occupation may be highly income-elastic. Thus increases in income will cause rents and house prices to rise (expect for very poor housing types), and quantities available to increase depending on price elasticities of supply.

INCREASES IN A AND FALLS IN F

The effect of these changes will be primarily to increase the demand for owner-occupied housing. As assets rise further, individuals will be able to afford deposits on a house and as interest rates fall, more will be able to afford the monthly repayments. The price of new houses will rise and more will be constructed. By virtue of substitution rents will also rise somewhat.

Returning now to the model, we can see that there are six equations to determine the six unknowns, r, P, S_r, D_r, S_o, D_o. One configuration of these is shown below.

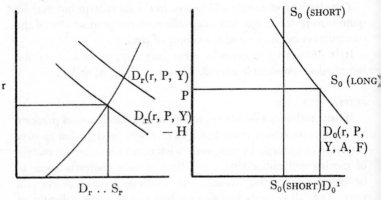

Fig. 12.

The private demand for new construction is shown as $D_o^1 - S_o$. The actual stock of houses for owner-occupation is S_o but the *desired stock* is D_o^1, i.e., it is the stock at which marginal demand price and marginal supply price are equal to one another. For the purpose of illustration long run supply price is taken to be constant.

HOUSING POLICY

The private demand for new construction is the difference between desired and actual stock. But the total demand for extra construction will be this private demand together with the number of new council houses that local authorities wish to build.

Suppose that total new construction demand is $(D_o^1 - S_o) + \Delta H$ where ΔH represents additional council houses planned. Normally it will take some time for the construction industry to meet this extra demand. If it can produce h houses at the most each year it will take

$$\frac{(D_o^1 - S_o) + \Delta H}{h}$$

years for equilibrium to be reached.

As presented, the analysis has assumed competitive equilibrium in the market for private tenancies. If, however, rents are set below the market clearing level, there will be excess demand for private tenancies. If, as we have been supposing, the supply of rented accommodation is price inelastic, the main effect will be to redistribute income from landlords to tenants, so tenancies will clearly have to be rationed by some other way than price. Whether or not frustrated renters will transfer their money demand to the owner-occupied sector will depend on whether those excluded are in high or low income groups. If they are in the latter, their natural alternative source of housing will be council housing and waiting lists will lengthen; meanwhile overcrowding will tend to increase.

Enough has been said to show that an effective housing policy depends partly on the planners' understanding of how the housing market works. The model presented is much too simple to be of direct use but gives a general idea of the qualitative effects of possible changes in the basic determining factors. It would be even better to have an idea of the quantitative effects. The evidence on elasticities of supply and demand for U.K. housing is rather thin, partly because the market is a regulated one in which observed positions cannot be assumed to be equilibrium ones. Thus American data is of interest. First consider income elasticity. A crude plotting of housing expenditure against total income shows that it rises much less rapidly than income and implies an income elasticity of the order of $+ 0.5$ or less. However, theoretical considerations tell us that expenditure on housing will be affected more by 'permanent' or 'normal' income than by current income. Once adjustment has been made for this it is found that income elasticities can be quite high, $+1.0$ or over.[1] Price elasticities seem to be of the order of -1.0. In other words, if permanent income rises by 10%, housing demand will rise by about 10% and if price rises by 10% housing demand will fall by about 10%. Recent U.K. estimates of the demand for *new housing* have suggested an income elasticity of $+0.7$ and price elasticities of the order of -0.3.[2]

Targets and instruments of policy

The targets of housing policy can be described in general terms as aiming to increase the housing stock, to improve its quality and to ensure that it is equitably allocated. More specifically, the targets might be to increase the housing stock to x million, to demolish y million houses and to ensure that the lower income groups pay no more than z% of their income for housing.

There are a great many instruments which governments may use to reach their targets. First consider government *subsidies* to housing. Notice that in the U.K. governments rarely act directly on the housing situation but rather through a very large number of local authorities. Local authority housing represents about one third of the housing stock and is subsidised by the central government (to the extent of £120 m.) and by local authority contributions to their own housing accounts (to the extent of £80 m.). Since the 1967 Housing Subsidies Act, the central contribution is calculated on the basis of the difference between the local authority borrowing rate and 4%. Clearly the central government may encourage or discourage local authorities by raising or lowering the subsidy. But the response to these variations is not at all reliable, for local authorities

---

1   R. Muth in A. C. Harberger, *Demand for Durable Goods*, Chicago, 1960. M. Reid, *Housing and Income*, Chicago, 1962.
2   A. E. Holmans, 'The Demand for New Housing', *Social Trends*, no. 1, Jan. 1971.

may often expand or contract their housing for ideological reasons. To this extent there is a case for establishing housing authorities independently of local government.

The purpose of building local authority houses is not, of course, simply to add to the stock of houses. It is to make sure that low income earners can obtain housing of a quality not obtainable in a free market at prices they can afford. Recent policy has been to raise council house rents to so-called economic levels and protect the lower-paid by a system of rebates. (In fact rents and rebates vary quite arbitrarily between local authorities.) The N.B.P.I. recommended in 1968 that rents should gradually rise to replacement cost levels and that the scheme of rebate suggested by the Ministry of Housing and Local Government in its circular 47/67 should generally be adopted. The main anxiety is that economic rents may be set rather too high. A good guide is the proportion of people entitled to their rate rebate—in many areas it is 25%; a figure of 50% would be rather absurd.

Owner-occupiers obtain a subsidy of the same order of magnitude as council house tenants in the form of tax relief on mortgage interest payments (£215 m. in 1969). This must have the effect of raising the demand schedule for owner-occupied housing and of redistributing real income from other classes of occupier to owner-occupiers.

The other main subsidy is in the form of generous grants for home improvements following the White Paper, *Old Houses into New Homes*, already referred to. Over 100,000 grants were given in 1969. The economics of renewal versus renovation are discussed later in this chapter.

A gap in the tax-subsidy structure, frequently commented upon, is the lack of direct subsidy to tenants in the private sector. There is no direct financial help for landlords except in the form of improvement grants and loans. Indeed some commentators have drawn attention to the relatively unfavourable tax treatment of landlords.[1] Instead the profitability of private landlordism has been curbed by

---

1   A. J. Merrett and A. Sykes, *Housing Finance and Development*, London, 1965.

POLICY

(gradually weakening) *rent control*. The details of rent regulation need not concern us. The 1957 Rent Act brought general decontrol but malpractice by landlords (including Rachmanism) led to the Rent Act of 1965. Under this act, the landlord or tenant could appeal to a rent tribunal for rent-adjustment, and tenants of unfurnished accommodation were given security of tenure. This security did not extend to furnished accommodation, which had the predictable result of a widespread switch to furnished letting as definitions of 'furnished' were not at all stringent. The rent tribunals were required to assess 'fair rents' but, in doing so, to avoid the element due to local scarcity. They have not in practice been able to follow this rather difficult directive and since 1965 fair rents have generally meant upward rather than downward adjustment. As their tendency to do so became known, landlords came to the tribunals in increasing numbers and landlords' applications soon outnumbered those of tenants.

The general principles of rent control have already been briefly discussed. Supply and demand analysis suggests two rather obvious effects:

(1) It will cause 'excess demand' for housing,
(2) It will discourage the supply of houses for renting.

The extent of the latter must depend on the price elasticity of supply. Because of both the relatively unfavourable tax treatment of landlords and political uncertainties, this elasticity will almost certainly be rather low. If this is so the effect of decontrol will simply be:

(1) To redistribute income from tenants to landlords and
(2) To stimulate a small increase in supply.

The contribution of the private landlord to housing has been so evidently in decline that one wonders whether it is either possible or desirable to arrest the fall. One way of stopping the decline would be to subsidise tenants directly. The present government has already announced its intention to extend the council house rent rebate

168

schemes to the private sector. The tenant would obtain a subsidy depending on the assessed fair rent and a means test. Others have suggested a more radical form of subsidy in the shape of housing vouchers which people would use to help pay for their accommodation.[1] The assumption behind all schemes of this kind is that rents would be allowed to rise to free market levels, supply thereby being encouraged. An equally likely result would be a straight transfer of income from the taxpayer to the landlord via the tenant.

Currently the most popular (and politically fashionable) type of reform is the facilitation of *mortgage borrowing*. At the time of writing, several modifications are being discussed. One of these is to follow the U.S. pattern of government underwriting or insuring certain types of mortgage—for example, where the property was old or where the repayments would be a large proportion of the borrower's income. Another is to introduce a rising repayment type of mortgage. Instead of the usual fixed annual payment the borrower would repay sums which would rise with his income and the general level of prices. The building societies have not traditionally looked kindly upon such schemes but they cannot be ruled out. A third method would be to subsidise mortgage interest rates directly to a greater extent than is done under the present option mortgage scheme. Under this scheme borrowers may opt to pay at 2% below the going mortgage rate but forgo their tax relief on mortgage interest payments. This scheme is attractive to those paying little tax and who do not expect their incomes to rise a great deal; it also becomes more attractive as the standard rate of income tax falls.

An increase in the housing stock helps all households even if it is concentrated at the upper end. But this depends on the efficiency of the so-called 'filtering' process (see next section). If it is very inefficient, those in the lower ranges of the market may benefit only a little. There is the further danger that if the housing construction industry is working nearly at full capacity financial aid to owner occupiers may simply cause house prices to rise.

---

1   See, for example, F. G. Pennance and H. Gray, *Choice in Housing*, Institute of Economic Affairs, H.M.S.O., 1968.

POLICY

Slums and the market

The allocation of houses among households depends partly on 'tastes' but mainly upon incomes. The higher a person's income the more he is likely to spend on housing. Thus, if there is a hierarchy of different quality houses people will be distributed among them roughly in the order of their incomes. Slum-dwellers will, typically, have low incomes; they will be able to afford only the poorest types of housing and will spend little or nothing on maintenance and repairs. Several policies with respect to slums are possible.

1. They can be pulled down with or without provision of alternative accommodation. Muth[1] has argued that slum clearance *per se* worsens the housing situation. It provides no alternative accommodation and creates pressure for upward movements in rents in slightly better housing types. Even worse, if slums are due to low incomes, they will tend to reappear after only a few years have lapsed (perhaps as little as six) as former slum-dwellers will continue to spend little on maintenance and repairs. The conclusions for policy of this line of reasoning are, of course, very pessimistic indeed.

If alternative subsidised housing is provided (the American term is 'public housing'), either for the slum-dwellers themselves or for others with whom they will come into competition, these pessimistic conclusions can be set aside. The argument surely must not be for a halt in the slum-clearance programme but for adequate and low-priced alternative accommodation.

2. Another policy would be to rely on some of the benefits of new house-building to *trickle down* to low income groups. Thus existing owner-occupiers move to out-of-town locations, existing occupiers of better class rented housing move into owner-occupation and so on, until some slum dwellers move into other poor rented accommodation and their slum houses are abandoned. A purely laissez-faire approach to the problem would be along these lines. But one could not expect rapid results from such a programme as the filtering process could be quite a protracted one, especially if there was

1   R. Muth, *Cities and Housing*, Chicago, 1970.

already overcrowding in medium to poor type rented accommodation. The easing of the situation at the top of the housing scale would be blocked and therefore fail to trickle down to the really deprived groups.

3. Income subsidies may be given to poor tenants. This would enable them to afford rather better quality housing and perhaps spend money on maintenance. The general principles of such subsidies have already been discussed. The objections to income subsidies are partly paternalistic (people may not choose what is good for them) and partly analytical. The analytical objection is that where the price elasticity of supply of cheap housing is low, an income subsidy will mainly have the effect of raising rents and redistributing income from tenants to landlords.

From this very brief discussion it is clear that neither slum clearance, filtering nor income subsidies can be effective solutions to the slum problem without an increased supply of middle- to low-range housing. A comprehensive policy for removing slums therefore requires a very active role by local authorities. Rather than the suburban council-housing type of development, one needs pockets of council houses as urban sites become available and acquisition of properties in poor states of repair owned by recalcitrant landlords.

To the extent that immigrant concentration and 'ghettos' are due to the lack of geographically dispersed cheap accommodation, an active policy along these lines would have a positive effect.

Building high

An additional grant given in 1961 to local authorities of £1·75 per flat per extra storey over and above six was abolished in the Housing Subsidies Act of 1967. Subsequently the Ronan Point disaster and wider appreciation of the difficulties of high living—in terms of stress and tension, inadequate lifts and play areas and experience of loneliness—have brought rather less enthusiasm for building high.

The economic rationale for high building runs in terms of saving land that is very expensive in central areas. The choice is between low density dwellings with low construction costs but high land costs, and high density dwellings with high contruction costs and low land costs. Everything being equal, the economic problem is to minimise the total cost of building a given number of dwellings of a given standard.

Type of dwelling	Construction costs (£)*	Land required per dwelling in acres	Total construction costs with land at (£)			
			5,000	10,000	20,000	30,000
2 storey flats	2512	1/10	3012	3512	4512	5512
3 storey flats	2991	1/30	3157	3324	3567	3991
6–8 storey flats	4464	1/50	4564	4664	4864	5064

*　From *Housing Statistics*, no. 19, Nov. 1970.

Land and construction costs of flats of various height

In the table, as land costs rise the higher types of building become more attractive. Thus by £10,000 per acre it has become cheaper to build three rather than two-storey flats. At £30,000 per acre three-storey flats are still best, but six- to eight-storey flats have now become cheaper than two-storey ones. Notice that the marginal cost of saving one acre seems to be of the order of £30,000 (a switch from three-storeys to six to eight-storeys saves 1/20 of an acre of land per dwelling but costs about £1,500 extra).

The conclusion must be that as a device for saving land, building high is not efficient unless land is valued very highly. The marginal cost is of the order of one hundred times the going price of good agricultural land. Even though this broad conclusion must stand, there are a number of ways in which its objectivity is questionable. Firstly there is the question of space requirements: these are very much as decreed by planners. But, if anything, these standards should be argued up rather than down, making high building an even more expensive way of saving land. Secondly, the cost of sites reflects zoning regulations and past planning decisions. The local opportunity cost of acquiring land for housing is the difference between the capitalised rentals of the displaced usage on that site and the capitalised rentals on a new site.

The knowledge that one does not save a great deal by building high is negative but useful in that decisions can be made on the basis of wider land-use policy. Taking into account congestion costs and its overall land-use/transportation plan to what extent does a local authority want to encourage housing on expensive central sites?

The analysis starts out as a cost minimisation exercise; but it soon broadens out into a fuller cost-benefit type of study.

Rebuilding or renovation?

Following the White Paper, *Old Houses into New Homes*, the government announced bigger grants for home improvement. The limits at the time of writing are £450 for the standard grant (provision of basic amenities) and £1000 for discretionary grants. A 50% discretionary grant is available of up to £1000 per flat if larger houses are converted. Some local authorities are relying heavily on the subsidy to induce owners in delapidated areas to improve the housing stock. An important adjunct to this policy is the establishment of 'general improvement areas' for which subsidies may be obtained to carry out work for the improvement of the environment.[1] The 1968 White Paper provided ample evidence that such money could be well spent. Thus 19% of dwellings lacked an internal water closet, 13% a fixed bath, 19% a wash basin, and so on. Some houses are in such a bad state that they should clearly be demolished and replaced; others have a long useful life ahead and should be renovated. Apart from the obvious cases, are there any general economic principles that bear on the decision? The important thing is not to take up a doctrinal position in favour either of rebuilding or renovation as a general principle without first understanding the relevant economic factors.

---

1   Part 2 of the Housing Act, 1969.

POLICY

The easiest way of setting out these factors is in terms of cost-benefit analysis. As usual, the money costs and benefits may be enumerated (see Chapter 9).

Renovation	*Rebuilding*
Benefits	
(1) Present value of extra rentals up to year of replacement	(3) Present value of (larger) extra rentals
(2) Present value of extra rentals after year of replacement	
Costs	
(4) Actual cost of renovation	(7) Actual cost of rebuilding
(5) Present value of rebuilding cost at replacement date	(8) Present value of larger reduction in repair costs
(6) Present value in reduction of repair costs	

Assuming a positive excess of benefits over costs for both programmes, the renovation programme is more likely to be chosen:

(*a*) the longer the length of life of the renovated property;
(*b*) the lower the cost of renovation relative to that of rebuilding;
(*c*) the less the extra repair costs on a renovated building compared with those on a new building;
(*d*) the lower the extra rental a new building would command;
(*e*) the greater the rate of interest.

Rebuilding is a capital-intensive activity relative to renovation; resources have to be committed at an earlier stage. At higher rates of interest the costs of *future* rebuilding will seem less important. Hence (*e*) holds.

Calculations such as these are sometimes done on a 'cost-effectiveness' basis only. It is assumed that benefits would be the same for either programme. Thus the only problem is to find the minimum cost programme.[1]

The items (1), (2), and (3) are not intended to refer simply to market prices but as reminders that at some stage the decision-

---

1 L. Needleman, *The Economics of Housing*, London, 1965, p. 203.

makers have to settle upon the relative values of a new and renovated property. Generally speaking, *ceteris paribus*, a renovated house would command a lower rent than a new house—but is it sufficiently lower to offset the cost advantages? Different rentals reflect different environments, different services, different shops and schools. More fundamentally the planners need to know how far people really do like to be rehoused in areas older but familiar to them. If we do not feel able to use market rentals as indicators of these preferences we must substitute planners' preferences supplemented by research into people's wants.

A cost-benefit study can therefore play a very useful part in the overall decision but it cannot supplant the value judgements of those in charge of policy. The conclusion that grants can be an effective way of halting the rate of deterioration of the housing stock does not, of course, mean that it is unnecessary to press ahead with the rebuilding of perhaps two million houses that are unfit. They are not a very useful weapon at the bottom of the housing scale. As grants are paid to owners, tenants cannot themselves carry out grant-aided repairs and even if they do, may well find themselves paying a higher 'fair rent'. Unless the bulk of the money is to go to middle-class owner-occupiers (with subsequent reliance on trickling down), local authorities will need to make more use of their powers of compulsion.

The 1968 White Paper showed that about one quarter of the housing stock required repair expenditure in the range £125–499. This is the range in which most grants operate.

Summary

It has been claimed in this chapter that economic analysis has a useful part to play in formulating housing policies, provided that the importance of planners' value judgements is recognised at various key points. The effectiveness of various instruments of policy cannot properly be understood without constructing models of how the complex housing market (or rather set of markets) operates. At various points it has been argued that local authorities have an even fuller part to play than at present.

17 INTERNATIONAL TRADE

Policy goals

Casual observation suggests that international economic policy (for a single country) could be formalised as follows:

Maximise (some measure of) real income subject to,
—avoidance of sudden economic or social dislocation,
—a balance of payments constraint,
—considerations of defence and international politics.

Though fairly realistic it is, as a policy criterion, rather untidy. It might take the form 'maximise the rate of growth of output subject to the constraints that the current account surplus[1] is not less than £100 m. and that employment in no industry falls faster than 1% each year.' To use this sort of criterion is certainly not 'irrational' unless all countries try to do so; it merely reflects the government's own set of value judgements.

A free trade policy is of particular interest because economic theory suggests that under certain circumstances it will enable a country to maximise its real income. Thus the *cost* of any trade restriction is a loss of real income. A government is perfectly entitled to modify the real income objective in all sorts of ways but it should be aware of the cost of each modification.

It should be clear from these introductory remarks that real income is at the centre of this chapter. Unfortunately the concept is not entirely straightforward and several things must be said about it. Firstly an increase in the index of real income constitutes only a 'potential improvement' as defined in Chapter 4. An actual improvement was defined there as a change such that someone was made

---

[1] The overseas accounts are drawn up so that the overall balance of payments equals zero. Thus, the net balance on current account *plus* net long term capital movements *plus* net short term monetary movements (including changes in reserves) = 0.

better off to nobody's detriment. The index of real income could, of course, go up at the same time as someone (say a worker in an import competing industry) became worse off. An increase in real income constitutes an actual improvement only if all losers have been compensated. That compensation is not likely to be paid *in fact* provides a rationale for combining some sort of social hardship constraint with the real income objective. It seems entirely just and humane to phase out a particular industry (coal is a good example) by a combination of natural wastage, retraining schemes, job availability elsewhere, incentives for other industries to set up in the area and a decreasing level of tariff protection.

A second point about the real income index is that it should take account of the future; strictly a measure of the *present value* of the real income stream over a planning period is required. This more sophisticated definition will be relevant in at least two cases, infant industries and overseas investment.

Thirdly, there is the question of whether policy makers are (or should be) interested in real income per head rather than total real income. This could be particularly important in deciding whether or not to allow freedom of factor movement in and out of the country or, more specifically, whether to allow uncontrolled immigration.

Fourthly, there is the question of how far policy makers wish (or should wish) to take into account the real incomes of other countries. This will affect their attitude to the trade problems of developing countries.

Maximising 'real income' is, therefore, not such a simple objective after all.

Trade and real income

For the purposes of this section, real income will be said to have increased when it becomes possible for a country to have (if it wishes) more of one commodity without having to have less of another.

It is a well-known proposition of trade theory that if, as between two countries, the structure of *relative* prices is different then it will be to the advantage of traders in both of them to undertake trade.[1]

Why should relative prices differ? We already know that under competitive conditions the forces determining relative prices are three: factor resources, tastes and production functions. As all of these may differ between countries it is hardly surprising that relative prices should differ. The main difference between pure theories of trade has been the stressing of one or the other of these forces. Thus the classical or Ricardian theory emphasised differing comparative costs (due to varying production functions) while the more modern Heckscher-Ohlin theory emphasised different factor resources (or endowments). Armed with a general equilibrium view of relative prices there is no need for us to be drawn into either camp.

The nature of the gains from trade can be seen with the aid of Figure 13. The curve of production possibilities is concave to the origin and shows the largest numbers of refrigerators and vacuum cleaners which it is possible to produce.

Before trade, the internal price ratio is 1 : 2 and efficient production is taking place at 'a'. During trade, the price ratio is 1 : 1·5 (see previous footnote). If resources are diverted from the production of refrigerators to the production of vacuum cleaners to a point 'b' and

---

1 A simple numerical illustration of the rudiments of international trade theory (of a type that goes back at least to J. S. Mill) may be helpful.

(a) TERMS OF TRADE. Let there be two countries, A and B, in which conditions are such that in country A

1 refrigerator exchanges for 2 vacuum cleaners

and in country B

1 refrigerator exchanges for 1 vacuum cleaner.

If there is to be any trade the *commodity terms of trade* must settle between the two ratios 1 : 2 and 1 : 1. The precise ratio established will depend mainly on demand conditions in the two countries. Suppose, for the sake of simplicity, that they settle at 1 : 1·5, i.e. 1 refrigerator exchanges (internationally) for 1½ vacuum cleaners. Let A export 15 million vacuum cleaners and B export 10 million refrigerators.

(b) EXCHANGE RATE. So far nothing has been said about the absolute levels of prices in A and B. Let vacuum cleaners exchange at an internal price of

INTERNATIONAL TRADE

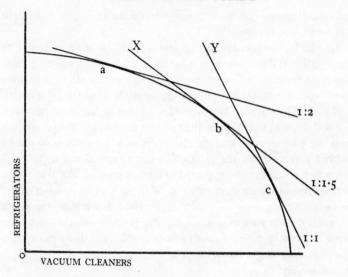

Fig. 13. The Gains from Trade

then vacuum cleaners are exported in exchange for refrigerators, it
will be possible to reach a point like X. At X real income is higher
than at 'a', as it is possible to have both more refrigerators and more

---

$2 in country A (the exporting country) and let refrigerators exchange at
an internal price of £1 in country B (again the exporting country). Then if
trade is to balance and there are no other transactions, A's exports to B
and B's exports to A must be equal in value, i.e.

A's exports = 15 m × $2 = $30 m
B's exports = 10 m × £1 = £10 m

Thus £1 = $3 is the equilibrium rate of exchange.

At any other rate of exchange trade would fail to balance unless, by
chance, there were several (multiple) equilibrium rates of exchange.

Notice that if *either* the underlying commodity terms of trade change *or*
if the absolute price level changes in either country, the exchange rate will
have to alter if equilibrium is to be maintained. Notice also that in order to
keep this illustration simple the 'real' and the 'monetary' parts of the
process have been kept entirely separate. More sophisticated models take
these interactions into account.

vacuum cleaners. (Even so, as has already been noticed, this might not be an 'improvement'.)

One further conclusion can be drawn from this short excursion to theory; that the increase in real income for a country will be greater the more favourable the terms of trade. If vacuum cleaners become more valuable in relation to refrigerators the country (illustrated) will gain. The terms of trade could not move beyond 1:1, however, for at that point the other of the two countries in our model will not find any advantage in trading. At a ratio of 1:1 resources would be further diverted into the production of vacuum cleaners (to point 'c') which could then be exported to reach a position like Y at which real income is higher than either at 'a' or at X. The division of the gains from trade between countries therefore depends on the terms of trade. *Ceteris paribus*, a small country is likely to gain most from trade because its internal relative costs are likely to differ more from the prevailing world terms of trade.

Summarising:

(1) The pattern of trade depends on the structure of relative prices.
(2) The gain from trade consists in an increase in real income.
(3) The division of the gains from trade depends on the terms of trade.

The balance of payments constraint

I have already said that it is not 'irrational' for a government to pursue objectives other than maximisation of real income. But the balance of payments constraint occupies a rather curious position. Unlike the need to prevent social dislocation or individual hardship or the need to pursue certain goals related to defence *even though* it means foregoing some real income, it cannot be argued that a balance of payments equilibrium at the current rate of exchange is *in itself* desirable and for which it is worth sacrificing some real income. On the contrary, making the balance of payments 'right' is often said to be a precondition of increases in real income. With this view the balance of payments is rather in the nature of an investment; forego some real income now to get it right and there will be higher real income in the future. In some less developed countries there may be cases where this is so. The balance of payments then becomes a policy instrument for achieving higher real income rather than a constraint upon it. But in advanced industrial countries this is not so. The real constraint is the rate of exchange. This is not the place for a detailed history of postwar exchange rates. It is sufficient to say that, after the Second World War, the non-communist countries adopted a system known as the 'adjustable peg', whereby each currency was pegged to the dollar which was in turn fixed in terms of gold. Only when a country's balance of payments went into 'fundamental disequilibrium' at the existing rate of exchange was a devaluation or revaluation of the currency permitted under I.M.F. rules. These periodic currency changes have been preceded by widespread speculation and attempts to avoid devaluation by reducing expenditure in the threatened countries and thereby reducing imports; i.e., exchange rates as a means of adjustment have been used only in the last resort.

Dramatic crises in the foreign exchange markets and attempts to hold back home expenditure (more than domestic considerations would justify) could be replaced by a system of 'flexible' exchange rates whereby the rate would move so as to bring about balance of payments equilibrium[1] at the going levels of prices and incomes. Most proposals along these lines envisage that in the short term the rate would be permitted to move only within a band but that this band would change (possibly at a pre-determined rate) over time.

To advocate more flexible exchange rates is not to suggest a painless cure. After a depreciation of the exchange rate imports become more expensive and exports cheaper; hence the terms of trade turn against the depreciating country. This deterioration is the real cost of altering the exchange rate and has to be compared with the costs (in terms of loss of output) of trying to hold the old exchange rate. The big advantage claimed for a flexible rate is that

---

1   It was said in a previous footnote that the balance of payments was always zero. This was, of course, because the change in reserves needed to bring it into balance is always included. It is in equilibrium when no change in reserves is required.

home economic policy can be directed towards domestic objectives and the balance of payments left to look after itself.

It might seem odd to the reader to be laying so much stress on what is, after all, merely a 'price'. But it is consistent with the philosophy of this book that prices are highly useful technical devices. One would naturally advocate a certain caution in changing over to a flexible rate and it might even be that the experiment would have to be abandonded (the old bogey of de-stabilising speculation and the off-chance that the import and export price elasticities of demand might be such as actually to worsen the trade balance). It would be worth trying flexible rates if only to escape from the present preoccupation with the balance of payments as almost the sole end of economic policy.

It is the author's view, therefore, that for an advanced industrial nation to treat its exchange rate as 'sacred' is foolish; but if it does wish to do so, the balance of payments policy constraint follows as a logical consequence.

Free trade and real income

So far we have seen that the policy goal of maximum real income may be constrained in various ways, some of them foolish and some not so foolish. Additionally, there are reasons why unrestricted free trade might *not* increase a country's real income.

Firstly, the set of relative prices (which, it will be remembered, determines the pattern of trade) may be 'distorted' in various ways. For example, certain types of medical service may be provided freely or at below cost for good social reasons, but it would be an inefficient use of resources to 'export' these services in the form of cheap medical care to foreigners. A similar argument applies whenever there is any monopoly element as this distorts the set of relative prices and therefore the pattern of trade. This general caveat is an example of the theory of 'second best' discussed in Chapter 10.

Secondly, there may be good macroeconomic reasons for wanting tariff protection. Real income might be low because employment is low. By protecting its own import-competing industries a country will be able to divert expenditure to them, thus increasing its general level of employment. This must be sharply distinguished from the 'phasing out' of a declining industry discussed earlier in this chapter. As a policy it might be inferior either because it did not work (owing to 'retaliation' by neighbours) or because better alternatives were available (conventional monetary or fiscal policies). Another, more likely, macroeconomic reason for wanting tariff protection is to enable the ('foolish') balance of payments constraint to be met.

The third technical objection is concerned with increasing returns (often known as the infant industry argument). There may be industries which are not competitive at present but are expected to be so once they have reached a certain critical size. Why do firms not grow to the crucial size? There may be constraints on the amount of capital expansion that firms are able to digest (for a discussion of this see Chapter 14). But, more importantly, efficiency is often a function of learning and time as much as of size. In this context the *present value of real income* concept is very relevant. Policy-makers are being asked to accept a reduction in current real income in return for higher real incomes in later parts of the planning period. Notice, however, that in Australia, where tariff protection is well established, economic opinion is moving in favour of selective subsidies instead.[1]

The fourth technical objection has to do with the terms of trade. If a country can turn the terms of trade in its favour it can (as we have seen) thereby raise its real income. The extent to which this is possible depends on the home elasticity of demand for imports and the foreign elasticity of supply of exports. In the extreme case of home demand being completely elastic the price to be paid for imports would fall by the whole amount of the tax! There would probably be some 'optimum' tariff that would secure the best possible terms of trade. (Torrens was, I believe, one of the first to point this out; see Chapter 5.) Most countries do, in fact, try to manipulate their tariffs in this way but the threat of retaliation (with world trade diminishing at each round) is a restraining factor. Another (though unfortunately weak) restraining influence is

---

1   See W. M. Corden, *Australian Economic Policy Discussion*, Melbourne, 1968.

altruism; there may be moral pressures at work to dissuade a government from manipulating its terms of trade against developing countries. From the point of view of the world as a whole the picture is rather different. The optimum tariff and beggar-my-neighbour arguments clearly do not apply; but the 'second best' and increasing returns arguments well might. Additionally a deliberately 'distorted' tariff structure might be an efficient way of redistributing real income towards less well-off countries (see later in this chapter).

Trade liberalisation

The general trend of postwar policy has been towards trade liberalisation. The General Agreement on Tariffs and Trade (G.A.T.T.) of 1947 has remained in force, though intended as a provisional device. Under its umbrella six rounds of negotiations have taken place on a multilateral, item-by-item basis. Following the postwar tariff cuts, a new proposal was made by the G.A.T.T. (1954) for across-the-board cuts of the order of 30% over a three year period. This ambitious plan was never implemented, mainly due to the opposition of Britain and the U.S.A.

The establishment of the European Economic Community (E.E.C.) or Common Market in 1958 was partly due to the failure of G.A.T.T.'s wider plan (the E.E.C. countries were France, Germany, Italy and Benelux). Following the collapse of negotiations for a broader free trade area the European Free Trade Association (E.F.T.A.) was set up in 1959 (the E.F.T.A. countries being Austria, Denmark, Norway, Portugal, Sweden, Switzerland and the U.K.). E.F.T.A. was a much looser arrangement than the E.E.C. in at least three respects and the striking difference in approach can be seen by glancing through the Treaty of Rome and the Stockholm Convention. The E.E.C. was committed to a common external tariff, to closer economic integration (harmonisation of tax rates, labour and capital mobility, etc.) and half-committed to eventual political integration. E.F.T.A. has no common external tariff and is regarded as a purely trading arrangement.

Economic theory suggests that freer trade in the context of a free-trade association or a custom union is less desirable than multilateral

INTERNATIONAL TRADE

free trade on a most favoured nation basis.[1] The reason for this is that tariffs will be discriminating as between members and non-members (this rather extreme form of discrimination is permitted under the G.A.T.T. article 24). Part of the trade that results from a customs union can be described as 'trade diversion'; trade between a country and its partner which would, in the absence of discrimination, have been carried on between that country and the outside world. In real terms, the country is worse off because of trade diversion. This adverse effect is normally reckoned to be more than offset by 'trade creation', so long as the external tariff is fairly low (trade that would not have taken place at all in the absence of the union).

In 1961 the U.K. applied to join the E.E.C. but the negotiations eventually failed due to the French veto. Meanwhile the Americans (as part of President Kennedy's Grand Design) passed the Trade Expansion Act of 1962 which aimed, among other things, at tariff negotiations with the E.E.C. as a whole (probably including Britain!). The American plan was for across-the-board cuts of 50% in the tariffs for most industrial products. Unfortunately a general formula for this type of cut could not be agreed upon and for various reasons the reductions actually achieved by the Kennedy Round (on the old multilateral basis) fell short of the original hopes. Cuts of 35% over the five years ending in 1972 were agreed upon.

At the time of writing active negotiations have just been completed for U.K. admission to the E.E.C. As for wider developments, it seems generally to be agreed by experienced negotiators that there is little room for more progress along the lines of the Kennedy Round. One (though limited) possibility is to take slightly further the industry-by-industry approach. Another is the strengthening of the E.E.C. (with or without the U.K.) along with some increase in protection by the U.S.A.; or perhaps a more 'liberal' E.E.C. including Britain. Yet another possibility is the formation of some sort of transatlantic open-ended association (often referred to as the North Atlantic Free Trade Area or N.A.F.T.A.). This would, in the first instance, include the U.K., Canada, the U.S.A. and the E.F.T.A. countries and eventually other Commonwealth countries, Japan and

---

1   Under m.f.n. there is no discrimination between countries.

perhaps the E.E.C. itself. It would be a much looser association than the E.E.C. The N.A.F.T.A. type of proposal is favoured only by an enthusiastic minority in the U.K. but has, apparently, some support in the U.S.A. and Canada. We must expect to hear a good deal more of it *whether or not* Britain joins the E.E.C.

It advocates such an association as a step towards trade liberalisation proper. Even though a free trade association is discriminatory, the bigger it becomes the more powerful it will be as an engine of free trade proper. Certainly both trade diversion and trade creation may increase. But if only a few countries remain outside the association there will be little trade diversion until, in the limit, it disappears altogether. Whichever way the direction of future liberalisation goes, a shift away from simple tariff reductions will be required in two major policy areas: 'non-tariff' barriers to trade and preferential treatment for developing countries. It is generally agreed that non-tariff barriers distort the pattern of trade and that 'harmonisation' of policies will be necessary. Some has already taken place within the E.E.C. and even the advocates of N.A.F.T.A. want sufficient harmonisation to be rid of the more obvious distortions. Essentially this represents methods of dealing with the second-best problem as discussed in Chapter 10.

Since the first United Nations Conference on Trade and Development (U.N.C.T.A.D.) of 1964, much more has been heard of the slogan 'trade-not-aid'. The developing countries have argued that trade liberalisation under the G.A.T.T., together with the trading associations of western Europe, has been almost entirely concerned with trade between advanced industrial countries. Reductions in the tariffs on electrical machinery, even when extended to developing countries, are of little use to them. Their real interest is in tropical produce and labour intensive manufactures (like cheap textiles) which tend to be excluded by quotas and prohibitions. Further, the commodity terms of trade turned against the developing countries (taken as a whole) by something of the order of 10% from the early 1950s to the mid 1960s[1] (i.e. they have needed to increase their

---

1 The reader should be warned that the meaning and interpretation of this figure is controversial.

exports by 10% merely to buy the same quantity of imports as before). Briefly, the developing countries argue that the whole trend of postwar liberalisation has in practice been discriminatory and that the balance should now be redressed. The trading needs of the developing countries cannot, however, be assessed independently of their other problems.

Factor movements

Alongside a liberal trading policy there should, logically, be a liberal policy towards factor movements. The classical theory of international trade was based on the simplifying assumption that factors of production were internationally immobile. *Within* a country we have already seen that free movement of factors assures, in principle, that factor rewards are everywhere equal at the margin and that, therefore, factor services are efficiently allocated. If factors are internationally mobile (and historical experience suggests that some of them are) it appears, by analogy, that their free international movement would enable efficient allocation from a world point of view.

This might achieve, more directly, what economic theory suggests *might* occur in the long run as a result of trade alone—the equalisation of factor prices. On the basis of that theory of trade (the Heckscher-Ohlin) which puts great emphasis on differing factor endowments, it is plausible that a country will export those goods which make intensive use of its abundant factor. Trade will tend to push its price up relatively to other factors so that, over time, factor rewards will tend to equality. (The conditions under which this *must* happen are very stringent.)

Consider labour migration. The causes of this are complex and include political and social influences as well as economic ones. But economic analysis suggests that a rational migrant will move only if he expects the present value of his lifetime income stream to be greater as a result. It is the expected difference in the earnings stream that matters (net of the actual cost of movement). Under perfect conditions the equilibrium distribution of labour will be such that the present value of the whole stock of labour is maximised. But no

POLICY

government (unless it is a world government) is interested in a *world optimum* labour distribution; such a distribution would be consistent on a large scale with depopulation and stagnation of certain areas.

It is in this context that a country's policy-makers may be interested more in maximising output per head (or per member of the indigeneous population) than in maximising total real income. Labour immigration will almost always increase output, and continuous immigration will raise the rate of growth of output but it may or may not increase output per head. In countries where there are greater and obvious labour shortages (as in postwar western Europe) labour immigration will almost certainly raise output per head but in general one cannot be sure. If a 1% increase in labour leads directly to a 0·8% increase in output, and to a further 0·2% due to economies of scale, output has increased altogether by 1% so that output per head remains unchanged. The stronger the economies of scale, the more likely it is that output per head will increase. 'Brain drain' is the mirror image of immigration. Under competitive conditions the world as a whole will gain but the 'exporting' countries will probably lose (though they may gain to the extent that increases in knowledge are, sometimes, world property and that the 'brains' return after a few years). Of course, to the extent that there are 'externalities', free factor movements will not maximise even world income (which is the same as maximising world income per head); but there is certainly no guarantee at all that free movements will assist the much more selfish objective of maximum income per indigeneous inhabitant.

Overseas investment, similarly, has the effect (in principle) of allocating new capital (or investment) in such a way as to maximise its present value. It therefore helps to meet a condition for the efficient allocation of world resources. Yet both initiators and recipients, intent on their own goals, frequently seem unhappy about it. The crudest objection in the initiating country is that capital is flowing out of the country and cannot therefore be used at home. But if the rate of profit earned abroad is greater than at home the present value of real income will be higher with overseas investment than without it. Only if investors are particularly foolish and unskilled would an objection be valid on this ground. But it may be that a country has included balance of payments constraint in its policy objective. Regardless of whether or not this constraint is foolish, it is true that, in the first instance, foreign investment does worsen the balance of payments of the initiating country. It would be quite rational in these circumstances to restrict overseas investment to a certain sum each year.

If important 'distortions' are present, unrestricted overseas investment might *not* lead to an efficient world use of capital. Two such distortions only are mentioned here (they illustrate once again the general difficulty of 'second best'): prohibitive import duties and differential tax policies. The effect of a protective duty on, say, motor vehicles may be that foreign firms set up assembly plants in the country thus 'jumping the tariff wall'. Australian policy provides plenty of examples of this. It might have been more 'efficient' from a world point of view to locate the plant in the investing country and then export to the protecting country. There may be no long term gain even for the receiving country. Given that protection involves some immediate loss of real income and therefore possibly lower domestic capital accumulation, the net amount of investment may be either greater or less than before. It all depends rather crucially on whether the foreign capital is of superior quality, embodying (as it is likely to do) a superior technology. Even the short term balance of payments gain could be sharply reversed as a result of profit repatriation.

Now consider differential taxes. A firm will normally be interested in maximising the present value of the resources it could invest *after tax* and will clearly choose a different pattern of investment than if it maximised present value *before tax*. But the latter, not the former, is relevant to the efficient allocation of resources. This is one reason why discussions of more liberal capital movements within the E.E.C. included discussion of harmonisation of tax policies.

Lastly there is the question of economic sovereignty (crystallised in European fears about the dominance of American firms). Various instruments of policy work rather less well when parts of industry are controlled from overseas; among these are prices and incomes policies, monopoly legislation and exchange control.

POLICY

Summary

It may or may not be in a country's interests to pursue a liberal international economic policy, even when its concern is simply to maximise (in some sense) its own real income. It may, of course, for various non-economic reasons wish to pursue policies that involve some sacrifice of real income.

It will be efficient for the world as a whole to pursue a liberal economic policy provided that 'distortions' of all sorts are removed at the same time (second-best). But, as we saw in Chapter 4, it may not be optimal to do so. This depends on one's value judgements about a 'just' world distribution of income and on the most efficient ways of bringing it about.

18 REDUNDANCY

At a superficial level technological progress has, apart from its aesthetic aspects and certain externalities, been entirely satisfactory from the economic point of view. As the main engine of economic growth it has raised per capita incomes beyond measure. But the attention of economic theorists and of the public has frequently been drawn to the possibility of technological unemployment, i.e., people thrown out of work as a result adopting of new techniques. This phenomenon can, in principle, be distinguished from unemployment due to an overall deficiency of demand and its victims are referred to as 'redundant' rather than 'unemployed'. An interesting nineteenth-century parallel is described in Chapter 5.

Our general welfare principle can be brought to bear. Automation or any other form of technical advance is a good thing if it brings about an *actual improvement*. It does so whenever it takes place without harming any one group or where the affected groups are fully compensated. Very often it will bring about only a *potential improvement*, that is to say, compensation could be paid but is not.

First it is necessary to define (in neo-classical terms) three types of technical progress. Let the overall annual rate of technical progress be $x\%$.

1. NEUTRAL

The marginal value products[1] of all factor services (including labour of type L) rise by $x\%$. Thus $x\%$ more output could be produced by the same bundle of services as before.

2. LABOUR-SAVING

The marginal value product of type L labour services rises by less than $x\%$ and of other factor services by more than $x\%$.

3. HEAVILY LABOUR-SAVING

The marginal value product of type L labour services actually falls and that of other factor services rises by more than $x\%$.

---

1   At the prevailing levels of all factor inputs.

POLICY

What would happen under competitive conditions? In case (1), wages, rents, etc., would all rise by x% and the share of type L wages in total income would therefore stay the same. In case (2), the marginal value product schedule of labour services would have moved to the right and the wage rate would increase *but* the share of wages in total income would have fallen. In case (3) the marginal value product schedule would have fallen to the left. Two conditions must be distinguished:

(*a*) Wage rates are 'flexible' as assumed implicitly above. The wage rate falls. The absolute earnings of type-L workers fall and there is a sharp redistribution in favour of the owners of other factor services. It might be necessary for wage rates to fall very low before a new equilibrium is reached and the progress might be painful and protracted (the handloom weavers, the 'Okies').

(*b*) Wage rates are 'rigid'. This is the spectacular case. The marginal revenue product schedule has fallen but the rigid wage rate means that employment has to fall. Essentially this is the Marxian outcome. This simple taxonomy suggests two things. Firstly, any type-L saving technical progress is immediately harmful to type-L workers and whether they become absolutely or just relatively worse off is a question of degree only. Secondly the form in which they are affected depends on how flexible wages are; the more flexible the greater will be the fall in wage rates and the less the unemployment.

Professor Meade[1] has recently directed the attention of economists to the economic and social implications of case (3*a*). The context is one where very labour-saving technical progress has caused the marginal value product of unskilled labour to decline. From the viewpoint of economic efficiency the wage rate should be allowed to decline (otherwise some labour will stay unused). In the extreme case, if the marginal product of unskilled labour were zero the wage rate should also be zero. But this solution has certain drawbacks. Meade suggests that interests of efficiency and of equity could be reconciled through the redistribution of property. A person's

---

1   J. E. Meade, *Efficiency, Equality and the Ownership of Property*, London, 1964.

income would then be made up of two parts, a wage (depending on the marginal value product of the labour services he could offer) and an income from property. Thus if widespread automation caused a fall in wages and a rise in profits it need not follow that income was unfavourably redistributed. It need hardly be said that there are strong arguments for this policy quite apart from the special case of technological unemployment. Meade argues persuasively for his solution as opposed to the 'trade union state' wherein a minimum wage would be fixed with either overt unemployment or work-sharing.

What of the longer term? Technical progress will increase total real income and this in turn will permit further economic growth and capital accumulation. As capital accumulates at a faster rate than population growth, the marginal product of all types of labour, other things being equal, will rise. The extent to which it rises depends on how good the new capital is as a substitute for labour. The less it can be used as a substitute for labour the more will the marginal product of labour rise. On this view the short-term effects previously described will have caused the curve of real incomes for type-L workers to 'hiccup' before resuming a now more rapid upward climb. It would be short-sighted to object to such technical advance merely because of short-term inconvenience. The welfare principle remains clear, however. Taking the planning period as a whole the potential improvement will be unequivocal; but if even a small group of workers lose in the very early years alone, the innovation will be only a potential improvement unless compensation is paid.

Marx was pessimistic on all these counts. There was no question of the (reproduction cost) wage rate adjusting so as to ensure full employment; technical progress took place at an ever-increasing rate and in great bursts (a prolonged bout of 'hiccups'); the growth of the 'reserve army' prevented any possible alleviation by means of a greater ratio of capital to total (as opposed to employed) labour. Marx uses the term 'relative surplus population' to describe the emergence of the reserve army.[1]

---

1   K. Marx, *Capital*, vol. 1, Moscow, 1867, p. 683 *et seq.*

POLICY

The decision as to whether to adopt a technical innovation is almost always a decentralised one; the decision-maker may be a profit-seeking entrepreneur or a Soviet enterprise manager. There may be genuine 'efficiency' reasons why it should not be adopted (it might lead to spoilation of the countryside or to atmospheric pollution) but in this chapter we are solely concerned with its effects on labour. Provided that there is a potential improvement, the aim of policy is to establish some means of turning it into an actual improvement. I shall consider just two types of measure, minimum wages and redundancy pay.

The labour market

The organised labour market is immensely complicated. For the purpose of this discussion I shall assume that wage rates are fixed as part of a bargaining discussion by trades unions and employers. The earnings of a typical industrial worker are made up of two parts, a 'basic rate' determined by industry-wide bargaining and a 'bonus' negotiated at plant level. (This has led some labour theorists to distinguish between the 'jobs market' and the 'hours market'.) The more sensitive component is the bonus; if workers are in short supply, if their productivity is unusually high or if conditions in the product market are good, the plant's shop stewards will be able to negotiate good bonuses. Earnings will be sensitive to marginal productivity differences, a feature which has caused many commentators to advocate more plant bargaining as being conducive to an efficient allocation of resources. (Notice that this argument collapses if the local union is able to exclude outsiders.) But these two levels of negotiation correspond to two types of decision—what is the appropriate wage rate in this plant relative to wage rates in other plants of the industry; what is the appropriate wage rate in this industry relative to wage rates in other industries?

Extreme advocates of the bargaining 'model' take the view that wage rates can be fixed anywhere within a very wide band, different wage levels simply reflecting different distributions of income between employer and employees. In a competitive model the 'band' is reduced to a single point, there is no choice. Now apply a 'bargaining' model to the technological unemployment case. The marginal value product of a particular group is, let us suppose, reduced; the union can insist that the previous wage be regarded as a *minimum wage* in that occupation and it can also (because the band is wide) insist on the old level of employment being maintained. In these circumstances Meade's criticism of the 'trade union state' solution would not apply.

Devotees of the middle way will, like the author, find it reasonable to assume that the upper and lower limits of the band are determined by conventional economic forces, that the upper limit is reduced when the marginal value product falls and that the bargaining solution is likely to be less favourable to labour as a result. The deterioration may, as before, take the form either of unemployment or of wage reductions, depending on the amount of wage-rigidity. Thus the presence of trades unions does not detract substantially from our initial conclusions about the effect of falling marginal value products on wage-rates and employment.

Policies

I consider minimum wage legislation unsuitable for dealing with the redundancy problem although it is admirably suitable in those parts of industry that are badly organised on the labour side. I base this judgement on the criterion of economic efficiency; to move labour from an activity where its marginal value product is low to an activity in which its marginal product is high usually constitutes a potential improvement. The alternative to minimum wages is redundancy payments plus industrial retraining.

The Redundancy Payments Act of 1965 provides for redundancy pay. This is independent of unemployment benefit and is intended to give workers financial security during the difficult period of transition from one job to another or to premature retirement. The Act gives a statutory right to redundancy pay in cases where workers are declared redundant or put on short-time working. Employers contribute to a fund out of which lump-sum payments are made depending on number of years of continuous employment and earnings while at work. Thus workers over eighteen with two years

POLICY

of continuous employment obtain a small payment while older workers with many years of service receive rather more. Failure to renew contracts as well as 'justified' walk-outs are also qualifications for payment. The Act represents an important advance of principle and has made some forms of unemployment less uncomfortable than formerly; but it is widely criticised as inadequate.

Additionally there is some provision for industrial retraining.[1] In 1960 government training centres (G.T.C.s) were established, principally for apprentices, the unemployed, ex-servicemen and the disabled. Though they enable workers to learn entirely new skills and to move across industry boundaries their scale is entirely inadequate, especially when compared with similar schemes in Sweden. Since 1966 they have moved over to retraining the newly redundant as well. Complementing the G.T.C.s, the Industrial Training Act of 1964 (something of a revolution according to workers in the field) set up training boards for whole industries, financed by levies on employers. Principally, these are concerned with training rather than 'retraining' but the emphasis is increasingly in this direction.

If technical progress is type-L-labour-saving, the marginal revenue product of type-L-labour will fall (absolutely or relatively) and if an *actual* improvement is to be effected type-L-labour must be compensated in some way. Ideally, one would like to be able to

1   The costs and benefits of industrial training can be classified as follows. (1) From the point of view of the industry total benefit is the present value of the extra 'value-added' due by industrial training. 'Value added' is a measure of the net output of the industry and equals wages, salaries, profits, interest, etc. Total costs are those borne by employers and employees in the industry. (2) From the point of view of the employer total benefit is the present value of the extra profit, etc., accruing to his firm as a result of extra training. Total cost is the cost borne by the employer either directly or in loss of profits, etc. (3) From the point of view of the employee the total benefit is the present value of the expected increase in his earnings due to the extra training. Total cost is the cost borne by the employee, either directly or in loss of earnings. As the employer is not normally able to bind the employee to the firm (in the manner of a slave) it will often be rational for the industry as a whole to carry out training that would not be carried out by individual employers.

196

compensate either for loss of income (where wages are flexible) or for loss of employment (where wages are more rigid) but it is very much easier, and more pressing, to do only the latter. Government measures of the last few years, principally redundancy payments and industrial retraining, have gone some way to provide such compensation.

The analysis of this chapter has been microeconomic, perhaps excessively so. The major cause of unemployment continues to be a deficient demand associated with policies designed to improve the balance of payments and moderate the pace of inflation. Some would argue that the threat of redundancy due to very labour-saving innovations is merely a 'scare', but it remains true that people do become redundant in particular industries and will need generous redundancy pay and efficient retraining.

Summary

Difficulties about technological advance arise from our social and economic forms of organisation. The essential point is that personal incomes are linked to the market value of labour services. As a long-term solution one requires a remedy like Meade's, i.e., redistribute property so that wages constitute only a part of each worker's total income. But in present circumstances this solution has a utopian ring about it. I have cast doubt on the use of minimum wage legislation to deal with this particular problem; it is likely to bring an inefficient allocation of labour and, in any case, technological change is no more likely to affect the very poorly paid than the better off.

BIBLIOGRAPHY : guide to further reading

CHAPTER 2

There are several good texts outlining the price system and the working of markets. I suggest one or more of the following four.

M. FLEMING, *An Introduction to Economic Analysis*, especially parts 1 and 2, London, 1969.

R. G. LIPSEY, *An Introduction to Positive Economics*, 2nd edn., especially part 2, London, 1966.

P. A. SAMUELSON, *Economics, an Introductory Analysis*, 8th edn., especially part 3, London, 1967.

G. STIGLER, *The Theory of Price*, 3rd edn., Chap. 1–11, New York, 1966.

A useful introduction to the application of econometric techniques to consumer and producer behaviour is

A. A. WALTERS, *An Introduction to Econometrics*, especially part 4, London, 1968.

CHAPTER 3

G. STIGLER (op. cit.), Chapter 17, provides a clear and simple exposition of the main theoretical principles of choice over time.

The pamphlet *Investment Appraisal* by the National Economic Development Council, H.M.S.O., 1967, gives a short practical guide to net present value to techniques.

A more detailed guide to the application of these techniques can be found in

A. J. MERRETT and A. SYKES, *The Finance and Analysis of Capital Projects*, London, 1963.

CHAPTER 4

The literature in this field tends to be a little heavy and difficult. Two basic texts are,

GUIDE TO FURTHER READING

J. DE V. GRAAF, *Theoretical Welfare Economics*, Cambridge, 1957.
I. M. D. LITTLE, *A Critique of Welfare Economics*, 2nd edn., Oxford, 1957.
E. J. MISHAN'S *Welfare Economics: 5 Introductory Essays*, New York, 1964, provides a more informal treatment.

A number of important but rather more difficult articles are reprinted in

K. J. ARROW and T. SCITOVSKY (eds.), *Readings in Welfare Economics*, London, 1969.

CHAPTER 5

The ideal recommendation is to try to read some of the classical writers themselves rather than commentaries. For general reference J. A. SCHUMPETER'S enormous *History of Economic Analysis*, London, 1963, is indispensable. See particularly part 3.

On the link between economic policy and political economy in the nineteenth century see

R. D. COLLISON-BLACK, *Economic Thought and the Irish Question*, Cambridge, 1960.
L. ROBBINS, *The Theory of Economic Policy in English Classical Political Economy*, London, 1952.
See also,
D. WINCH, *Economics and Policy: A Historical Sketch*, London, 1969, for an account of economic policy and the Keynesian Revolution.

CHAPTER 7

The following three articles on externalities are reprinted in *Readings in Welfare Economics* (op. cit.).

J. M. BUCHANAN and W. C. STUBBLEBINE, 'Externality', *Economica*, 1962 (NS 29).
J. E. MEADE, 'External Economies and Diseconomies in a Competitive Situation', *Economic Journal*, 1952 (62).
T. SCITOVSKY, 'Two Concepts of External Economies', *Journal of Political Economy*, 1954 (17).

BIBLIOGRAPHY

CHAPTER 8

The Penguin Modern Economics Readings *Public Enterprise* is very accessible and almost every article in it is worth reading. It is edited by R. Turvey, 1968.

The reader might also like to dip into J. MARGOLIS and H. GUITON, *Public Choice: A Book of Readings*, London, 1969.

A relatively recent and important statement of policy is to be found in *Nationalised Industries: A Review of Economic and Financial Obligations*, Cmnd. 3437, H.M.S.O., 1967–8.

There is also a regular stream of reports from the House of Commons Select Committees on Nationalised Industries.

CHAPTER 9

M. E. BEESLEY and C. D. FOSTER, 'The Victoria Line: social benefit and finance', *Journal of the Royal Statistical Society* (A), 1965, part 1.

This is a 'classic' and should be read as a pioneering work in this country.

Two useful general surveys of the whole field of cost-benefit are

R. S. PETERS, *Cost-benefit Analysis*, Institute of Economic Affairs, Eaton Paper no. 8, 1969 reprint.

A. R. PREST and R. TURVEY, 'Cost-benefit Analysis: A Survey', *Economic Journal*, 1965.

A valuable guide to practitioners with many simple examples of application is,

P. B. KERSHAW (ed.), *Cost-benefit analysis in Local Government*, Institute of Muncipal Treasurers and Accountants, 1965.

Finally see the recent report of the Roskill Commission which has brought a certain amount of (largely) unfavourable publicity to cost-benefit analysis.

CHAPTER 10

The literature on second-best is rather technical although the general principle is clear enough.

GUIDE TO FURTHER READING

A good early introduction is to be found in J. E. MEADE'S *Trade and Welfare*, part 2, pp. xii-xv.

The classic statement is in

R. G. LIPSEY and K. LANCASTER, 'The General Theory of Second Best', *Review of Economic Studies*, vol. i. (24), 1956-7.

A recent, but not clearly resolved theoretical dispute, was contained in the *Review of Economic Studies* of July 1967. Some of the basic issues remain to be sorted out.

These articles are advanced and fairly mathematical.

CHAPTER 11

G. F. HADLEY provides a straightforward introduction to the techniques in *Linear Programming*, Reading, Mass., 1962. The fat volume by R. DORFMAN, P. SAMUELSON and R. SOLOW, *Linear Programming and Economic Analysis* (London, 1958) shows the relevance of linear programming to most parts of economic theory. See also,

W. J. BAUMOL, *Economic Theory and Operations Analysis*, 2nd edn., New Jersey, 1965.

J. R. HICKS, 'Linear Theory', *Economic Journal*, 1960.

H. MAKOWER, *Activity Analysis and the Theory of General Economic Equilibrium*, London, 1957.

CHAPTER 13

On the earlier period see

A. ERLICH, *The Soviet Industrialisation Debate 1924-8*, Cambridge, Mass., 1960.

If, like the present author, the reader has to rely on English language writings, access to very recent developments is difficult. The following two books provide a good theoretical and empirical background.

A. NOVE, *The Soviet Economy: an Introduction*, 2nd edn., London, 1965.

P. J. D. WILES, *The Political Economy of Communism*, London, 1962.

BIBLIOGRAPHY

For the controversy over price reforms see

E. G. LIBERMAN, *Planning, Profit and Incentives in the U.S.S.R.:*
1. *The Liberman Discussion*, ed. M. E. Sharpe, New York, 1966.

CHAPTER 14

For the background to 'behavioural' theories of firms see

J. G. MARCH and H. A. SIMON, *Organisation*, New York, 1967 reprint, and

R. M. CYERT and J. G. MARCH, *A Behavioural Theory of the Firm*, New Jersey, 1963.

Two, by now, classic attempts to create a more general theory of the firm are E. PENROSE, *The Theory of the Growth of the Firm*, London, 1959, and R. MARRIS, *The Economic Theory of Managerial Capitalism*, London, 1964. Penrose, as her title suggests, emphasises growth as the main goal of firms while Marris stresses the role of managerial discretion and the stock market.

Two readable and wide-ranging accounts of western capitalist business are:

J. K. GALBRAITH, *The New Industrial State*, London, 1967 and
A. SHONFIELD, *Modern Capitalism*, Oxford, 1965.

Detailed accounts of specific industrial situations are to be found in the reports of the Industrial Reorganisation Corporation and the Monopolies Commission referred to in the text.

CHAPTER 15

A stimulating, but rather diverse, set of Fabian views is contained in *Social Services for All?* parts 1–4, by PETER TOWNSEND *et alia*, (Fabian Tracts 382–385) 1968. For an exposition of the 'free market' view, see J. M. BUCHANAN, *The Inconsistences of the National Health Service*, Institute of Economic Affairs, Occasional Papers 7, H.M.S.O., 1965.

GUIDE TO FURTHER READING

The H.M.S.O. publication, *Economic Trends*, periodically gives estimates of the *Incidence of Taxes and Service Benefits* (see for example Feb. 1969).
See also the following,

B. ABEL-SMITH, *The Poor and the Poorest*, London, 1966.
A. B. ATKINSON, *Poverty in Britain and the Reform of Social Security*, Cambridge, 1969.
C. V. BROWN and C. A. DAWSON, *Personal Taxation, Incentives and Reform*, P.E.P. Broadsheet 506, Jan. 1969.

CHAPTER 16

The best general introduction is D. V. DONNISON's *The Government of Housing*, London, 1968.
L. NEEDLEMAN gives a rigorous introduction in *The Economics of Housing*, London, 1965.
A. J. MERRETT and A. SYKES, *Housing Finance and Development*, London, 1965, contains currently relevant proposals for financial reform.

The following book is invaluable for any reader who wishes to take a deeper interest in housing,

P. A. STONE, *Urban Development in Britain: Standards, Costs, Resources, 1964–2004*, vol. 1, N.I.E.S.R., 1970.

CHAPTER 17

A solid standard text is C. P. KINDLEBERGER, *International Economics*, 4th edn., Homewood, Illinois., 1968.
B. BELASSA provides one of the few good accounts of the effects of tariff reductions in *Trade Liberalisation Among Industrial Countries*, London, 1967.
H. G. JOHNSON, *World Economy at the Crossroads*, Oxford, 1965, is a stimulating and wide-ranging collection of essays.
R. PREBISCH, as secretary, calls for a radical reassessment of trade policies towards developing countries in U.N.C.T.A.D.'s *Trade Prospects and Capital Needs of Developing Countries* and in earlier publications.

BIBLIOGRAPHY

CHAPTER 18

H. R. KAHN, *Repercussions of Redundancy*, London, 1964.

This gives a detailed empirical account of the experiences of those declared redundant.

J. E. MEADE, gives a modern 'liberal' view of what should be done in conditions of very labour-saving technical progress in *Efficiency, Equality and the Ownership of Property*, London, 1964.

MARX'S own account of the reserve army of unemployed and relative surplus population can be found in *Capital*, vol. 1, Ch. 15, Moscow, 1867.

INDEX

205

INDEX

INDEX

INDEX